*The Sonnet
Over Time*

UNIVERSITY OF NORTH CAROLINA
STUDIES IN COMPARATIVE LITERATURE

Number 63

WERNER P. FRIEDERICH, *Founder*
DIANE R. LEONARD, *Editor*

Editorial Board
EDWIN L. BROWN
ALFRED G. ENGSTROM
EUGENE H. FALK
ALDO D. SCAGLIONE
JOSEPH P. STRELKA

The Sonnet Over Time

A STUDY IN THE SONNETS

OF PETRARCH, SHAKESPEARE, AND

BAUDELAIRE

Sandra L. Bermann

The University of North Carolina Press
Chapel Hill and London

© 1988 The University of North Carolina Press
All rights reserved
Manufactured in the United States of America

Library of Congress Cataloging-in-Publication Data
Bermann, Sandra, 1947–
The sonnet over time: a study in the sonnets of Petrarch,
Shakespeare, and Baudelaire / Sandra L. Bermann.
p. cm.—(University of North Carolina studies in
comparative literature: no. 63)
Bibliography: p.
Includes index.
ISBN 0-8078-7063-3 (alk. paper)
1. Sonnet. 2. Petrarca, Francesco, 1304–1374—Criticism and
interpretation. 3. Shakespeare, William, 1564–1616—Criticism and
interpretation. 4. Baudelaire, Charles, 1821–1867—Criticism and
interpretation. I. Title. II. Series.
PN1514.B43 1988   87-37220
809.1'42—dc19   CIP

The paper in this book meets the
guidelines for permanence and durability
of the Committee on Production
Guidelines for Book Longevity of the
Council on Library Resources.

92 91 90 89 88   5 4 3 2 1

Portions of Chapter 1 are reprinted by permission of *Romanic Review*, vol. 72, no. 2, March 1981, pp. 215–25. Copyright by Trustees of Columbia University in the city of New York.

A part of Chapter 3 first appeared in *Proceedings of the Xth Congress of the International Comparative Literature Association, New York, 1982*, ed. Anna Balakian. New York: Garland Publishing, 1985, pp. 7–11.

"Swarthy when young; who took the tonsure; sign," from *Berryman's Sonnets* by John Berryman. Copyright © 1952, 1967 by John Berryman. Reprinted by permission of Farrar, Straus & Giroux, Inc., and Faber & Faber, Ltd.

To my mother and father

Contents

Acknowledgments ix

Introduction 1

Chapter One
Lyric Metonymy: The Petrarchan Sonnet 10

Chapter Two
Dramatic Metaphor: The Shakespearean Sonnet 51

Chapter Three
Referential Irony: The Baudelairean Sonnet 93

Conclusion 142

Notes 153

Bibliography 163

Index 169

Acknowledgments

In completing this book, I have benefited from the counsel of many colleagues and friends. I owe the genesis of the project to conversations and courses with James Mirollo and Pellegrino D'Acierno at Columbia University. James Mirollo read the manuscript and advised me at many points along the way, and for his friendship and expertise I am deeply grateful. I also wish to thank my colleagues at Princeton, Ralph Freedman, Earl Miner, and Suzanne Nash, all of whom offered discriminating criticisms of the manuscript along with heartening encouragement. Robert Hollander made several important suggestions, now thoroughly integrated into the chapter on Petrarch. I much appreciate his comments, as I do those of a more distant colleague, Eléonore Zimmermann, who cast a careful critical eye on the chapter dedicated to Baudelaire. To Robert Fagles who, over the years, has maintained his faith in me and in this manuscript, I owe a special debt of thanks.

My work has been greatly assisted by generous research leaves from Princeton University as well as a welcome subvention from the Research Committee, and by the opportunity to teach many talented students interested in lyric poetry and literary criticism. My particular thanks to Carol Szymanski for her care in typing the manuscript and to Diane Leonard who, as editor of this series, proved to be unfailingly patient and helpful. To my husband George, who somehow made time in his busy schedule to read the manuscript and to offer his incisive advice, I owe the greatest debt of all.

Introduction

Why revisit the sonnet? A form born and bred in the literary past, it is one that scarcely sets today's lyric fashion. Often enough, it evokes poetic, historical, and philosophical assumptions no longer our own. Yet this venerable form, once imagined, has never ceased to be written, even to our own day, and has so powerfully shaped the image of what lyric poetry is as to be, at times, practically equated with it. In fact, scarcely a major poet since the fourteenth century—writing in Italian, French, German, Spanish, or English—has omitted the sonnet from his or her repertoire. A good number have given it a central place. Such vitality alone makes the sonnet a continuing mystery. What is the function of its fixed verse form—the two quatrains and sestet of the Italian and French and the three quatrains and couplet of the Shakespearean? What sort of semantic range does this short lyric permit? What might account for its unusual longevity? And what might the sonnet be able to tell us about the long lyric tradition in which it so prominently figures?

A major premise of this book is that lyric language is language used to reach beyond ordinary assumptions and perceptions, to open up new vistas of world and self. In this view, poetry remains a revolutionary force in language regardless of its attachment to any genre or tradition. In fact, what emerges above all from a study of the sonnets of three poets as widely separated in literary history, national tradition, and poetic style as Petrarch,

Shakespeare, and Baudelaire is the lyric's enormous potential for difference.

REPETITION WITH A DIFFERENCE

Differences—semantic, stylistic, or phonic in nature—can be particularly striking in the sonnet since the form itself is so closely bound by repetition. After all, what makes a sonnet? Its generic definition usually announces little more than a series of repetitions: fourteen hendecasyllabic lines rhyming ABBA, ABBA, CDE, CDE (the most common Italian form) or fourteen iambic pentameters rhyming ABAB, CDCD, EFEF, GG (the Shakespearean). Such formal descriptions literally turn on the frequency and complexity of repetition. If meter is that regular repetition of accent and syllable by which we mark the temporal patterning of a text, rhyme is the repetition of sound tying one word to another, usually at the end points of each line, and stanzas organize repetition of rhyme and meter into larger units. The sonnet, with its brief, closed form and its intricate patterns of meter and rhyme, might well be said to emphasize, even to epitomize, the repetitive qualities at work to some extent in every lyric poem. That the sonnet is considered a major lyric genre and that it belongs to a centuries old tradition suggests that repetition is at work here on a particularly large scale.

Repetition is not absent from other literary forms; different genres employ it more or less obviously. For example, in traditional narrative, where linear, developmental, and cause-effect processes dominate, repetitions of image and theme continually cross the story's progress. They unify it and, at the same time, lend it new levels of complexity. Thus, in Stendhal's *La chartreuse de Parme*, the charterhouse itself may enter the narrative only in the final clause of the penultimate sentence. But a series of closely related images—the belfry tower, the paternal castle, and the prison tower of Parma—lace the plot so fully with the motif of monastic enclosure that the single reference to the charterhouse would seem, in the abstract, practically pleonastic. In fact, it allows the episodic story to be grasped as a complex unit whose images foreshadow without foreclosing the narrated action of its hero.

But the traditional versification associated with fixed verse forms, of which the sonnet is but one example, employs repetition far more pervasively, or at least far more obviously, than the novel. The regular recurrence of meter and rhyme seals a sonnet off from less organized writing, all the more so as the effect is magnified by the appeal of repetitions to the eye as well as to the ear. Stanzaic units trace visible patterns on the page that phonic repetitions only further embed. Within these visual and phonic bounds, meaning arises. It is tempting, in fact, to identify the sonnet almost totally with its repetitive elements.

Still, the sonnet, for all the importance of its repetitions, distinguishes itself by the play of differences—those inscribed within its bounds as well as those separating individual renditions of the form over time. For instance, from its origins in the thirteenth century, the sonnet has been characterized by the very asymmetry of its repetitions. Unlike the medieval *canso*, whose stanzas repeat one another using the same form and melody, the self-standing sonnet contains first an octave, whose eight lines are based on one pattern of repetition, and then a sestet, with a different rhyme scheme, to create a complex, formally self-conscious pattern. Its interest lies in the difference beween lines 8 and 6 or 12 and 2, a specifically sonnetlike difference-within-repetition. Then there are those differences that a poet can instill to express his or her unique lyric vision. In the hands of Petrarch, Shakespeare, and Baudelaire, such differences within and between renditions of the form are molded deftly, sometimes dramatically.

At times, the sonnet's formal repetitions seem to be used merely to create tensions in the text, against which other, equally powerful forces work. Petrarch's sonnets, for instance, with their logical development of thought, their emphasis upon grammatical figures, and their extensive use of complex hypotactic sentences, stress linguistic features that frequently run counter to the sonnet's repetitive form. And, in the process, the phonic and semantic effects of the repetition of rhyme recede in importance. In the sonnets of Shakespeare and Baudelaire, elements of repetition serve instead as the most visible sign of the poem's process of meaning. Repetitions not only create form but, in very dramatic ways, heighten the power of language to open itself to semantic differences—new images, concepts, feelings. Shakespeare's sonnets, for example, carry a chain of metaphors, puns, and lexical ambiguities in which the repetitions of the sonnet's form themselves play a particularly important role. In the sonnets of Baudelaire, repetitions of meter and rhyme are perhaps even more "differential." If, on the surface, the Baudelairean sonnet seems static in its structure and in its imagery, its complex similes and allegorical figures actually depend on emphatic differences of space and time inscribed in its syntax.

But regardless of how repetition—and difference—are used within the sonnet, a text so brief leaves all too little time to develop broad themes fully. At most, a single poem can indicate the direction that an elaborate lyric treatment might take. Surely one of the principal fascinations of the sonnet is just this tendency to leave its fictions inconclusive and indeterminate, with enough indications to trigger a reader's imaginings, but not so many as to close them off.

Nowhere is the sonnet's ability to play upon difference as well as repetition so thoroughly marked as it is in the sonnet sequence or the lyric book. Here we find repetitions of similar but hardly identical texts, whose interlocking similarities and differences create the imaginative world so pronounced in the three lyric collections I have considered here. Although widely diverse in character, Petrarch's *Rime sparse*, Shakespeare's *Sonnets*, and Baudelaire's *Les fleurs du mal* all play upon the sonnet's capacity to remain at once a closed formal structure and, at the same time, a mere fragment of a much larger, more open, lyric statement. Within collections such as these, the sonnet can exceed its usual bounds, producing a variety of narrative and descriptive effects generally restricted to longer verse or prose forms. Gathering separate sonnets into a larger group allows identifications to arise, identifications of figures, of names, of characters. And along with these ultimately come images of a poetic self—its attitudes, its situation—that together serve to focus the developing lyric text.

For repetition not only helps to organize texts or events, to create poetic form and genre. It also helps re-present. In a literary text, words seem to repeat or stand for something external to them, which the reader goes on to imagine. In the lyric, with its concentration of first person pronouns and deictics that together gesture toward a moment and source of the utterance, the element the reader fictionalizes most powerfully is generally the poetic persona, the voice of the text. Presenting itself variously—more or less distant, sincere, questioning, meditative—this image of a lyric self serves to organize, even to ground with its apparent authority, the other images of the poem. As one poem follows the next in a lyric collection, this poetic persona establishes itself more fully in the reader's mind.

In the lyric sequences examined here, a personalizing language, with a constant reference to "I," is most noticeable in the verse of Petrarch and Shakespeare. Though inevitably haunted by heterogeneity, the poetic voices of both these authors strive toward some prominence and stability. By contrast, the sonnets of *Les fleurs du mal* conjure an alienated and fragmented self, an effect that, ironically, ends only by evoking that problematic voice more forcefully in the reader's mind. At times, in the apparently nonrepresentational universe that Baudelaire paints, the identity of the persona seems to escape complete disintegration only through the very presence of formal and thematic repetitions. It is a self for which repetition helps provide a final, if illusory, stability.

In the elegantly shaped sonnet and the full sequence, we thus see a play of repetition and difference that focuses our attention on literary form—and, equally important, on the fiction of an individual voice. According to Paul Oppenheimer, this "introspective, quieter" mode that the sonnet seems to engender with its carefully crafted form, was its very birthright.[1] Certainly it characterizes most of the sonnet writing of the next seven centuries.

GENRE AND GENEALOGY IN THE SONNETS OF PETRARCH, SHAKESPEARE, AND BAUDELAIRE

Given the enormous range of poets who have written successful, even brilliant sonnets, the reader has every right to ask: why choose to study those of Petrarch, Shakespeare, and Baudelaire? True, countless poets could serve as the center for this inquiry into the sonnet. But I have chosen these three precisely because they so well exemplify how highly individualized and fully differentiated a single, apparently circumscribed genre can be. Working within a fixed form notable for its finely tuned repetitions-with-a-difference, and also within a literary tradition that came into being precisely through knowing repetitions of this form through time, each of these authors still creates a strikingly individual sonnet style. Through readings of the three poets, I attempt to describe their rhetorical differences, distinctions so dramatic that I have turned to different rhetorical terms to name them.

Employing some twentieth-century rhetorical definitions as well as insights drawn from much earlier periods, I have called Petrarch's style metonymic, Shakespeare's metaphoric, and Baudelaire's ironic and allegorical. The rubrics themselves are intended as no more than figures for the lyric idioms I attempt to describe. That is, they are themselves understood to be repetitions of sorts, with no claims to finality, but only to a rethinking of poetic possibilities.

Of course, to venture beyond the figure metaphor when describing the rhetoric of poetry is to refuse to repeat a major romantic notion that still clings: namely, the view that metaphor and especially symbol, are the defining properties of poetry.[2] In fact, a close inquiry into poetic rhetoric soon reveals the limits of such a perspective. Though highly tropological, poetry may—and does—range quite widely from the symbol and metaphor our Romantic heritage enjoined upon it. By examining the works of three sonnet artists, I hope to emphasize the differences in the rhetoric of the sonnet genre and thereby underscore some of the differences animating all of what we call lyric poetry. I hope that by delineating three distinct rhetorical tendencies, I might add some differential breadth to the traditional way in which we view the rhetoric of poetry.

But how do these differences arise? Though much of the rhetorical uniqueness of each author's work has to do with innate poetic gifts and inclinations, such talents are themselves subject to the literary, linguistic, and historical situations in which he writes. In short, through the synchronic differences of poetic style I have so far emphasized emerges another theme equally necessary to relate: the historical.

Not surprisingly, the five centuries from Petrarch to Baudelaire entail much literary, cultural, and linguistic change, very little of which can be included in a short and focused study such as this. Still, the repetition of the sonnet form throughout this long period does provide a convenient lens for highlighting one small current within a more extensive lyric history. For if the sonnet's form is severe in its disciplined repetitions of meter and rhyme, its repetition over time offers an author the important poetic advantage of strong and immediate historical resonance. And through the sonnet's inevitable echo of previous texts, the writer also gains an opportunity to assert the relative modernity of his or her own individual voice. In this way, the repetition of form through time brings with it both tradition and change.

Still, the task of description is not an easy one. What we call the sonnet tradition is reducible neither to a simple linear course nor to a clear-cut picture. Much like the artful form of the sonnet itself, tradition actually implies space as well as time, difference and similarity. Over the course of time, the sonnet tradition gathers definitional space through conventions of exchange and complicity that make literary tradition as much a community or a state as a genealogical line. It gathers laws and ideologies. And, like the larger social state of which it is a part, literary tradition breeds its own discontents, seeking to revolutionize it. Even the most scrupulous adherent, determined to respect a prior model through repetition and thus to live well within the literary establishment, invariably commits a treason against it, merely by refracting his or her ideal through the recalcitrant matter of language. The contingent, complicating facts of a more general literary history also enter into the relationship of filiation that might exist between any two poets' work. In the case of the sonnet tradition, a few such facts can be outlined here, as they frame the more specific relationship of one text, one poet, to another.

The long history of the sonnet tradition peaks in the fourteenth to sixteenth centuries, then falls, to rise again only in the nineteenth.[3] It flourished with the Renaissance and, somewhat less dramatically, with the Romantic and Symbolist movements. Not incidentally, both periods saw dramatic transformations in poetics and notions of self. The growth of the sonnet's popularity parallels the rise of Renaissance humanism, when classical texts and, with them, the Greek and Roman emphasis on human individuality and distinctive literary styles, gained new importance. With the Renaissance, in fact, grew the still familiar notions of "author," (as the person holding authority over the meaning of a book), "literature," "reading public," and "work of art." The sonnet contributed directly to these developments.

If Petrarch and Shakespeare neatly frame this initial moment of the sonnet's popularity, Baudelaire, on the other hand, writes at a time when the clarity—even the existence—of categories such as these begin to be questioned. The renewed quest for spirituality and the self that characterizes the late nineteenth and early twentieth centuries brings with it a new emphasis on lyric forms such as the sonnet, but also an introspective questioning that undermines previously accepted truths about poetic subjectivity and literary expression.

As we look to the sonnets of Petrarch, Shakespeare, and Baudelaire, we will note how such literary and historical issues contribute to sonnet styles that, though repeating what has come before and thus assuring the lineage of the sonnet form, also assert each poet's difference. Throughout the five centuries between Petrarch and Baudelaire, the sonnet's formal features remain strikingly similar. It takes on the quality of a special idiom and, at times, even a dominant mythology within the conventional language of poetry. But each of these three poets, while building upon the past, manages to create a special place for himself, to make himself "modern" in the context of his immediate predecessors and contemporaries. In short, each poet uses the sonnet to fulfill its differential, as well as its repetitive, potential. The differences are enough to leave their impact not only on our view of the sonnet but, one could hazard to say, on our view of the lyric tradition as a whole.

Chapter One

Lyric Metonymy
The Petrarchan Sonnet

Solo e pensoso i piú deserti campi
vo mesurando a passi tardi et lenti,
et gli occhi porto per fuggire intenti
ove vestigio human l'arena stampi.

Altro schermo non trovo che mi scampi
dal manifesto accorger de le genti,
perché negli atti d'alegrezza spenti
di fuor si legge com'io dentro avampi:

Sí ch'io mi credo omai che monti et piagge
et fiumi et selve sappian di che tempre
sia la mia vita, ch'è celata altrui.

Ma pur sí aspre vie né sí selvagge
cercar non so ch'Amor non venga sempre
ragionando con meco, et io co llui.
—Sonnet 35[1]

"Solo e pensoso" is one of Petrarch's most anthologized sonnets, and for good reason. Through its musical, self-reflexive patterns, it subtly presents some of the poet's most distinctive effects. Its logical train of thought seems at first to move in a weary circle. A poet-lover seeks the most deserted paths, shunning all eyes that might discover his passion. But his solitary walk brings him straight to "Amor," that ubiquitous other who is, of course, but a projection of the speaker himself. By the end of the poem we know that no effort to escape spares the poet this painful and, as the verb phrase "venga sempre ragionando" suggests, this continual self-speculation.

The cyclic pattern of troubled meditation, ending less in resolution than in impasse, strikes a familiar chord in Petrarch's lyric collection. The theme of constant and contrary striving echoes briefly in other sonnets and receives a fuller orchestration in several longer canzoni. For instance, the quest for peace conceived in Christian terms struggles repeatedly with more earthly desires. In "I' vo pensando" (canzone 264) the second stanza asks:

> Se già è gran tempo fastidita et lassa
> se' di quel falso dolce fugitivo
> che'l mondo traditor può dare altrui,
> a che ripon' piú la speranza in lui,
> che d'ogni pace et di fermezza è privo?

But, as the canzone proceeds, other thoughts remind the poet of the two "knots" that tie him to the world. First there is fame:

> Da l'altra parte un pensier dolce et agro,
> con faticosa et dilectevol salma
> sedendosi entro l'alma,
> preme 'l cor di desio, di speme il pasce;
> che sol per fama gloriosa et alma
> non sente quand'io agghiaccio, o quand'io flagro,
> s'i' son pallido o magro;
> et s'io l'occido piú forte rinasce.

Then, equally powerful, the attractions of love:

> Ma quell'altro voler di ch'i' son pieno,
> quanti press'a lui nascon par ch'adugge;
> e parte il tempo fugge
> che, scrivendo d'altrui, di me non calme;
> e 'l lume de' begli occhi che mi strugge
> soavemente al suo caldo sereno

> mi ritien con un freno
> contra chui nullo ingegno o forza valme.

But like "Solo e pensoso," the canzone does not reach a decision; it simply continues the discourse:

> chè pur deliberando ò vòlto al subbio
> gran parte omai de la mia tela breve;
> né mai peso fu greve
> quanto quel ch'i' sostengo in tale stato:
> ché co la morte a lato
> cerco del viver mio novo consiglio,
> et veggio 'l meglio, et al peggio m'appiglio.

We might take the comparison further, from Petrarch's poetry to his most confessional work, the *Secretum*. A dramatization of yet another encounter, between the figure Augustinus (a rather Senecan version of Saint Augustine of Hippo) and Franciscus, a figure of Petrarch himself, the *Secretum* largely concerns the poet's struggle with *acedia*, an insufficient vigor in loving God and the good. Weighed down by a desire for fame and love, pictured here as "chains" rather than "knots," Franciscus is not able—in a sense not even willing—to rid himself of them, and his introspective soul-searching, in striking contrast to the Augustinian experience it plainly evokes, remains unresolved.[2] Though at times he may regret his earthly love for Laura, he never does extinguish it. Still less does he stop writing about her or seeking fame through his lyrics. In this broader Petrarchan context, the sonnet "Solo e pensoso" typifies a central Petrarchan theme of restlessness ending in impasse; Contini's description of Petrarch's poetics seems to fit precisely: a fundamental "assenza di moto."[3]

But helpful though it is, Contini's reading, with its emphasis on stasis, still leaves room for critical reflection. It is incomplete and, to some extent, even deceptive. Though Petrarch's sonnet may lack the decisive drive of a sonnet by Dante or Shakespeare, it nonetheless possesses an inner energy of which Contini's characterization does not take account. Pulsing through its style as well as its themes is a humanistic counterpoint to the medieval

Christian solution—namely, an historically ground-breaking urge to create through language a strong poetic "self." It is this self-dramatization, perhaps more than anything else, that accounts for Petrarch's critical identification ever since the Renaissance with a highly subjective, even "confessional" poetry.[4] Although such an urge for poetic self-creation is never a simple matter and, in fact, expresses itself in complex, even ambiguous ways, its power within the *Rime sparse* is unmistakable. It can be said without exaggeration that this power will energize the sonnet tradition for centuries to follow.

Petrarch was not, of course, the first to write sonnets. By the fourteenth century, when he composed his collection, an important sonnet tradition already existed, with distinctive forms and a repertoire of love themes. The earliest sonnets were born with the burgeoning literature in the vernacular, at the close of the Middle Ages, the first known examples written by a group of Sicilian poets called the "scuola siciliana."[5] Arising at a time when rules of versification were bound to rules of rhetoric, and accepted phonic and even musical patterns were deemed as essential to poetic expression as its series of consecrated themes, the sonnet appears to have been an invented and artistic rather than popular form. It was created by Giacomo da Lentino and other prominent courtiers of Frederick II.

The sonnet thus made its debut in a particularly opulent and forward-looking court, the one that produced the earliest translations of scientific and philosophical material from Arabic and Greek, enjoyed secular libraries, and fostered the growing prestige of vernacular poetry.[6] In such a setting, the sonnet attracted attention as a sophisticated native form. It stood out from contemporaneous lyric patterns through its asymmetrical, single stanza shape that, apparently, resisted musical accompaniment.[7] Certainly, as Giacomo used it, the sonnet was well suited to displays of virtuosity and meditative themes. And already, it revealed the characteristic octave-sestet division, with its turn of thought at line 8 that eventually became standard. It elegantly shaped some of the prevalent courtly love themes, such as praise of an idealized lady and the uplifting effects of a "servizio d'amor" that, with revisions and qualifications, would remain central to the sonnet tradition well into the Renaissance.[8]

Before the sonnet came to Petrarch's attention, it had in fact passed through the hands of the leading poets of thirteenth-century Bologna and Florence: Guido Guinizelli, Guido Cavalcanti and, especially, Dante Alighieri. Each was noble by birth, but the sonnet, at least as these poets developed it, did not serve merely to entertain the court. Its private, meditative potential suited it for introspective reflections or, more importantly, for the verse epistle. As such, it contributed to the first major Italian school of poetry, the "dolce stil novo." Growing outside any feudal court, almost as if in contrast to the ongoing competition between nobles of the day and the newly wealthy merchants, this literary school forged an intellectual alliance, based upon similar ideals for the emerging vernacular literature and similar thematic approaches to secular love. If Guinizelli established some of its founding principles through his canzone, "Al cor gentil"—which defined nobility purely in intellectual and moral terms—poets such as Guido Cavalcanti, Lappo Gianni, and Dante Alighieri refined the sonnet's Italian pattern and gradually transformed courtly love themes into more individualized expressions of secular love. Eventually, Dante became their head.

In his linguistic treatise, *De vulgari eloquentia,* Dante describes the sonnet as a popular form, compared with the more noble canzone.[9] Yet his poetic practice often belies his theory. Dante did write a number of poems, including the so-called *Rime petrose,* whose sensual subject matter conforms little to his own standards of poetic nobility. But precisely in his youthful lyric collection, the *Vita nuova,* where the sonnet appears in force, he reaches beyond the limits he himself established for the form. Though the sonnet is not the only poetic genre here—the sequence also offers several other lyric forms and connecting prose passages—still, in Dante's hands, it does stand out through an unusual linguistic simplicity and thematic depth. Sonnets such as "Tanto gentil" elaborate themes of erotic and spiritual love unique to the lyric tradition, in which the beloved Beatrice already seems less the ideal courtly lady than a sign of God. Grouping such sonnets with canzoni, ballate, and prose passages, the *Vita nuova* develops an inspired expression of love that finally refers the reader to the broad Christian themes that Dante would pursue in the *Divina commedia*. But in the course of the much slighter *Vita nuova*, Dante creates a lyric collection whose narrative line and emphasis upon a love experience both individual and universal in significance, offers important material for later versions of the sonnet. In the process, and in seeming contradiction to his evaluation of the form, he established it as an eloquent lyric expression.

From a strictly chronological and geographical point of view, Petrarch, writing in the fourteenth century, could hardly avoid choosing the sonnet for at least some of his own Italian lyrics. Supported through most of his life by aristocratic families in the wealthy Italian city-states, Petrarch traveled frequently on diplomatic missions or wrote at his country home in Vaucluse, near Avignon. In both the Italian states and Provence, the sonnet was by now an established—and important—vernacular form.

Petrarch was also deeply influenced by (though publicly unappreciative of) Dante, particularly his use of the lyric collection. It is virtually certain, as Robert Durling suggests, that Petrarch created the *Rime sparse* with the *Vita nuova* in mind.[10] But by using a collection of lyrics to depict not the miracle of a God-ordained love but the earthly, vacillating psychology of a lover, Petrarch abandoned the medieval Christian inspiration of Dante's lyric book to inscribe in his own verse a problematic nostalgia for a different and then relatively unknown world—the classical—in which the human subject played a more central role. Through his selection of a highly Latinate vocabulary and syntax and his use of the lyric collection as a self-reflexive, indeed a self-creative device, Petrarch attempted to capture values of the classical past in the growing vernacular idiom. In so doing, he took a major step away from the medieval symbolic framework in which his immediate predecessors had written, and toward what we now associate with the modern lyric.

Not that this step was taken lightly. As we have begun to see in "Solo e pensoso," the inner tension between a need for spiritual peace and an attachment to earthly, and therefore transient, desires makes his work the portrait of a particularly difficult, historically novel quest.

Certain clues to Petrarch's revolutionary poetics lie within the poem "Solo e pensoso" where, as we have seen, the poet seems to draw us into a thematic cul-de-sac. But the very process by which he does so—a dramatic transformation of the image of self and the external world—helps reveal the dynamic self-dramatization at work in his introspective poetics. Initially, nature—its "campi" and "arena"—stands fully external to the poet, a refuge from those who might perceive his love. As self-anatomizing figures of speech make abundantly clear, the action of the lover ("passi tardi et lenti," "atti d'alegrezza spenti") would easily betray his inner state to any observer. In fact, there is someone observing the wanderer in this lonely landscape. It is none other than the poet-lover himself—subject of the verbs, and also contemplated object in the pronoun "mi" and in the more distanced, third person forms "gli occhi" and "atti d'alegrezza spenti."

Curiously, such passive self-observation continues only until line 8, when the perspective changes suddenly. Just at the sonnet's turn, the poet turns the relationship of poet to nature inside out. First, a dramatized self steps forward with the (grammatically unnecessary) first person subject pronoun ("io") and the intransitive verb "avampi" (both in line 8). This emphatic self-concentration (underscored in line 9 through the subject pronoun "io" and reflexive verb "mi credo") prepares a thematic turnabout that also changes nature—from a protective shield to a reflecting mirror. In this transformed world, itself aware of the speaker's inner turmoil, how can we wonder that "Amor" finally emerges? Less an external myth than a crystallization of the poet's own emotion, "Amor" changes solitude to dialogue—"et io co llui"—a dialogue with the self.

Such a thematic transformation, drawing a world outwardly observed into a lively inner scene, is practically a hallmark of the Petrarchan sonnet. Still, it is but one sign of the introspective turn that shapes several dimensions of Petrarch's poetics. Building upon an unusual "visibility" of style, a number of poetic devices draw the artistic maker, vacillations, uncertainties and all, to the reader's attention.

VISIBLE GRAMMAR

For centuries, rhetoricians have divided figurative language into "figures of grammar" on the one hand, affecting the logic and arrangement of words, and "tropes" on the other, producing changes of meaning and usually limited to one or a few words.[11] Though this distinction clearly may be questioned,[12] it does cast some light on the unusual importance granted to syntax in Petrarch's style. The long sentences of the sonnet "Solo e pensoso," for instance, present a number of so-called grammatical figures: inversions (lines 1, 3, 4, 13), a postponed adjective (line 3), and an ellipsis (line 14).

An emphasis of this magnitude on syntactic design definitely affects the reader. Though grammatical figures cannot be dissociated from changes of meaning, they convey a change in a way that never allows us to forget their form. Interwoven patterns set the poem into relief as visible words—both a graphic design and a puzzle of meaning to be worked in the mind.

Such carefully wrought yet sometimes quite imageless "ragionamenti" doubtless helped earn Petrarch De Sanctis's title "artista, non poeta." They might even have been what prompted the fifteenth-century satirical poet, Francesco Berni, to label Petrarch's poetry a style of "words" as opposed to Dante's or Michelangelo's style of "things."[13] This last distinction should perhaps be exhumed for the sake of its largely accurate observations. But, I would argue, the value judgment it carried should remain interred. Is visible grammar, a "rhetorical" awareness of words, necessarily antithetical to poetry? At worst it is. At best, it may represent a different type of poetry, one highly appropriate to its historical moment and its lyric purpose.

As post-Romantic readers attuned to modern poetry, we tend to associate the poetic almost exclusively with images created metaphorically, to look for a set of analogies and oppositions that produce an invisible, imaginative world so brilliant it obscures our awareness of language and syntax as such. Still, at other moments of literary history, or for poetic reasons different from our own, a lesser emphasis on the metaphoric need hardly indicate a fall from the literary. It may rather mark a turn to what we would call today a more metonymic, more grammatically focused, style.

Jakobson's distinction between metaphor and metonymy offers a useful reference point here, since it implicates both the grammar and semantics of a literary text and highlights the complexity of any stylistic description according to trope. In the original, full-length version of "The Metaphoric and Metonymic Poles,"[14] Jakobson bases his definition of the two styles on a binary understanding of language and semiotic practice. Following Saussure, Jakobson calls one axis of language the "syntagmatic," and identifies it with the linear flow of words (and sounds) that exists *in praesentia* and is characterized by combination and contiguity. The opposing axis of language, the "paradigmatic," takes in the associative expanse of the reader's and speaker's minds. This realm, which encompasses the entire available linguistic "code," exists (from a linguistic point of view) in absentia, in the mind alone, and is characterized by relationships of similarity and opposition. Drawing on an older rhetorical tradition as well as on clinical studies of aphasia, Jakobson uses the terms metaphor and metonymy to describe stylistic emphases on one or the other of these two linguistic axes.

According to Jakobson, a literary text emphasizing the metaphoric will build its imaginative world through similarity and opposition, by selecting, repeating, and substituting, to create analogies and antonyms. Exploiting these possibilities of language (all associated with the so-called paradigmatic axis), the metaphoric style takes the reader quite naturally, and even inevitably, beyond the words on the page to possibilities of meaning that lie beyond them. Such an emphasis upon substitutions of meaning highlights what we might call poetry's "cognitive" dimension,[15] informing the reader about the world—real or imagined—that the poet engenders through his imagery. In such a style, the linear track of words recedes in our efforts at abstraction and substitution as we grasp the novel meanings. This stylistic tendency gains a fertile semantic dimension through the correspondence Jakobson draws between it and the effects of symbolization and identification described at length in Freud's *Interpretation of Dreams*.[16]

The case is markedly different for the metonymic style, which tends rather to exaggerate the play of contiguity and combination. It is not just a style that uses the tropes metonymy and synecdoche (themselves requiring less abstraction, less distance from a literal understanding of words than metaphor), but one that underscores the characteristics of the syntagmatic and thus the flow of grammar and syntax as they appear *in praesentia*.[17] Its emphasis on the order of words and meaning, rather than the analogical substitution of new meaning for old, leaves the text itself more visible, and stresses the linear drive of meaning, its movement from one word, one figure, to the next. Focused no more on the world created than on the grammatical forms that bring it into being, the metonymic, especially in the hands of a great stylist such as Petrarch, accentuates language as the rhetorically persuasive performance of its speaker. Although it too elicits a semantic comparison with Freud's study of dreams, it finds its parallel in the psychic devices of condensation, displacement, and, as subsequent critics have added, in the affiliated notions of postponement and deferral that characterize desire.[18]

Though the metaphoric has come to be associated regularly with poetry and the metonymic with prose, the emphasis placed on this division is, I would argue, more a mark of our post-Romantic heritage and a pleasure in neat categorization than of anything else. The almost exclusive attention given to metaphor in twentieth-century criticism derives not only from the fact that we have a better vocabulary to describe it, but also from metaphor's ability to suggest a poem's identity, self-sufficiency, and ontological presence, all of which well suit the idealist bases of most twentieth-century American criticism. But metonymy, with its more linear, discursive series of displacements, has often had a place in poetry and, more recently, in literary criticism.[19]

I would like to suggest, then, that if a strong metonymic ten-

The Petrarchan Sonnet / 19

dency is the way of least resistance for prose, it may also mark a strictly poetic path. It is certainly more apt to assert itself in Latin or in a classically inspired Italian verse, with their frequent plays on the order of words, than in modern French or English poetry, with their preconceived notions of lyric's stake in metaphor. An unusually strong reliance on the metonymic is, I believe, one of the defining qualities of Petrarch's poetry. His frequent use of the figure metonymy and the closely related synecdoche; his development of a complex, often involuted syntax and grammar; moreover, a development of meaning that stresses the power of a voice to build a logical or narrative argument, all mark a strong metonymic penchant. Even Petrarch's themes—from the systematic displacement of Laura to the unending desires of the lover, to the very difficulty of establishing a stable, ontologically "present" self—all evoke a metonymic description.

Still, as Jakobson makes clear more than once, and as subsequent theorists have explored to great effect, no linguistic tendency is perfectly metonymic or metaphoric, neither simply performative nor solely cognitive.[20] In literature, as in any language act, both tendencies are continually at work. To describe a text as metaphoric or metonymic is merely to suggest an emphasis, not an exclusivity. The elasticity and complexity of the classification, elaborated in Genette's study of Proust[21] and De Man's meditations in *Allegories of Reading*,[22] must certainly be retained in our inquiry into Petrarch's verse. For who would ignore the metaphors of the *Rime sparse*—the well-regulated web of images as well as the metaphoric allusions to classical texts? But, as we shall see, Petrarch finally curbs the independent power of the metaphoric. He yokes it firmly to a syntactically vivid discourse and a poetic quest as metonymic in its themes as in its style.

In the light of these comments, let us return briefly to the sonnet, "Solo e pensoso." Here, we find Petrarch employing a grammatically rich, metonymic style—but judiciously. Elaborate syntactic play occurs throughout, making the reader continually focus on contiguity and context. But particularly in the first part of the poem, we are faced with inversions evoking Petrarch's Latinate models and highlighting his own sophisticated artistry. The figures metonymy and synecdoche dominate here too, where they transform the self into a series of objects and events that the poet (and reader) can observe. But as the text proceeds, metonymy builds to metaphor—though of a characteristically Petrarchan sort—when, at the sonnet turn, the poet depicts the solitude and power of his love.

I say characteristically Petrarchan because the metaphors suit a rhetoric reluctant to elicit a brilliant external world, images that might eclipse, even for a moment, the speaking voice in charge of the rolling, almost Ciceronian periods. Petrarch curbs metaphor's mimetic re-presenting power in several ways. Most obviously, he embeds metaphoric images within a highly visible syntax, so that they must always compete with artful patterning for the reader's attention. Equally important, he builds them mostly from specific sorts of noun-verb rather than noun-noun interactions, transforming categories and classifications but seldom engendering altogether new concepts by coupling two vastly different words or images in the reader's mind.[23]

For instance, in the tercets of "Solo e pensoso," nouns depicting the natural world combine with the human connotations of "sappian" to render a personification. But if the landscape thus gains from metaphor its mythic dimension, it still never escapes from the poet-speaker's perspective. If anything, it approaches it more nearly, through its newly "human" qualities. Similarly, in the final lines, the abstraction "Amor" gains substance from the animating verb "venga," but without gaining the power to greatly distract the reader from the artful persuasion of the speaker's discourse, which comes to its elliptical end here.

And what sort of vision do these closing metaphors reveal? Though the Romantics and also Petrarch's great predecessor Dante might turn to metaphor to transcend the human,[24] to capture a glimpse of the infinite in the fallen language of humanity, Petrarch uses metaphor to imply the invisible and spiritual in a much more limited sense. Whatever imaginative leaps his metaphors offer draw but the confines of the persona's own psyche. Contained and controlled, metaphors serve to make it more palpable.

One need not search too far to discover possible sources for

Petrarch's preference for an intensely visible discourse. The mainstream of fourteenth-century love poetry, with its roots in both Provençal and classical lyric, generally elaborated upon a fixed series of situations and images, all dealing to some extent with themes of courtly love.[25] In this tradition, variation rather than novelty gave proof of poetic *virtus*. But Petrarch's variations were unusually pathbreaking, and they were so, in part, because of their more evident classical inspiration.

Unlike many of his predecessors, Petrarch was not content to be a troubadour whose work might—or might not—some day emerge in written form. Nor was he seeking through his poetry a solely religious transcendence. A man who composed a letter to posterity in fine classical style, Petrarch firmly believed in his earthly, historical importance. As he read the Roman poets and polished his rhetoric according to classical norms,[26] he looked expectantly to the time when he too would be acknowledged as a great man of letters. A poetry accentuating its written, artistically elaborated qualities, much like those observed in the classical Latin texts he read would, he doubtless thought, provide a fitting vehicle for his immortality.

Petrarch's classical inspiration led him to transform the lyric vocabulary then available. He did not follow in Dante's footsteps, seeking out contrasting "voci," words with different histories, various provenances—Florentine, Provençal, classical, contemporary dialects, neologisms. Instead, in the light of his classical preferences, Petrarch progressively refined what has aptly been termed an *unilinguismo*,[27] an extreme homogeneity of primarily Latinate words. Such a carefully pruned lexicon leaves room for variety but highlights artful syntactic and sonoral combinations.

As we have begun to see in "Solo e pensoso," Petrarch's visible style, with its grammatical figures, its metonymies, synecdoches, and carefully yoked metaphors, finds its primary role in projecting the speaker's psyche itself onto a highly visible plane, subject to clear-cut analysis and appreciation. It is a way of drawing into prominence the performing artistic maker, the sonnet's voice.

Moreover, as Petrarch could not have failed to note, a visible grammar firmly enlists other readers in its restless movements. Unable—and unwilling—to escape the snares of Petrarch's well-wrought periods, the reader follows the often hypotactic, often suspended discourse on and on in direct imitation of the poet's metonymic themes of an endless discourse on an endless love. Never resting in a fully viewed image, the reader's mind journeys forward, itself desirous of the next, contiguous word, restlessly seeking something, someone stable to contemplate. But in the context of the *Rime sparse* this goal must remain forever out of reach. Instead of an end and a fullness of meaning, the reader finds postponement, deferral, and desire, the semantic complements of the involuted metonymical visible grammar we have so far noted. The quest itself, with its dramatized, highly visible poet-questor, takes center stage. If we ask what he seeks, we find that the answer must begin with Petrarch's very choice of words and, especially, with the word "Laura."

"LAURA" OR SELF-REFLECTION

As readers of the lyric know, poems often use words to elicit immediate, powerful images that can be seized as real in some sense. Such a use of language—one that accentuates its potential to translate external things and bring them brilliantly before the mind's eye—corresponds to a basically mimetic, Aristotelian notion with which Petrarch was doubtless well acquainted, if only through his readings of Dante's *Commedia*. But for his hundreds of lyrics, almost all written about the beloved Laura, Petrarch chose instead a singularly abstract vocabulary—one that does not represent so much as continually distance, displace, and fragment. Consider the words of sonnet 246, for instance, that begins with a play on Laura's name:

> L'aura che 'l verde lauro et l'aureo crine
> soavemente sospirando move,
> fa con sue viste leggiadrette et nove
> l'anime da' lor corpi pellegrine.

> Candida rosa nata in dure spine,
> quando fia chi sua pari al mondo trove,
> gloria di nostra etate? O vivo Giove,
> manda, prego, il mio in prima che 'l suo fine:
>
> sí ch'io non veggia il gran publico danno,
> e 'l mondo remaner senza 'l suo sole,
> né li occhi miei, che luce altra non ànno;
>
> né l'alma che pensar d'altro non vòle,
> né l'orecchie, ch'udir altro non sanno,
> senza l'oneste sue dolci parole.

Here, we find a number of typical Petrarchan nouns—"l'aura," "lauro," "crine," "viste," "anime," "corpi," "rosa," "mondo," "gloria," "etate," "fine," "danno," "sole," "occhi," "luce," "alma," "orecchie," "parole." Lacking vivid denotative power, these tend to produce a lyric world filled less with immediate sensuous things than with distanced, contemplated concepts of things. A vocabulary of this sort, evoking a select Latinate past most aptly characterized by Augustine's psychological description of words as "thoughts of things,"[28] could leave its reader feeling detached and indifferent. But Petrarch uses it cannily, to create a "language within a language" that ostensibly describes Laura, but, through different sorts of indirection, actually inscribes image after image of the poet's desire.

To make the task of creating a highly individualized style and self-centered meaning somewhat more manageable, Petrarch limits himself to a surprisingly small number of words, and he colors their meanings in various ways. Repetition alone sometimes serves the purpose. This is the case with certain words, metaphors, and comparisons (some chosen from traditional figures) that recur so relentlessly, so imitatively, that it is tempting to call Petrarch himself the first Petrarchist. For instance, "sole" serves as a metaphor for Laura so frequently in the *Rime sparse* that eventually it suggests her almost automatically. Petrarch now and then complicates the reader's response by adding other references, allowing "sole," for instance, to designate Apollo or, occasionally, God. But what is most striking is that through its repeated figurative usage, "sole" neither refers to the natural sun, nor does it conjure a vivid imaginative world. It remains distanced and carefully defined according to poetically motivated repetitions.

But the web of meaning responsible for portraying Laura and the poet's love for her is frequently woven by other means. Notable among them are metonymic associations of sound and sense. The first line of "L'aura che 'l verde lauro," for instance,—where a breeze ("l'aura") gently moves the mythic laurel tree ("lauro") and a golden mane of hair ("l'aureo crine")—finds Petrarch using words that merely suggest, rather than attempt to represent, Laura through a form of paronomasia. The adjective "l'aureo" refers to the gold of Laura's hair while the two nouns evoke separate imaginative spheres apparently external to her, but associated with her as her setting and, like "l'aureo," echoing her name. In this way, repetition of sound actually eases a metonymic displacement of Laura into the two semantic fields—nature and myth—that, throughout the *Rime sparse*, serve as her context. The overall effect is complex. On the one hand, as Laura's golden hair blends with the breeze and the laurel, the woman is subtly displaced into a range of associated poetic themes. On the other hand, similarity in sound undermines each separate image, making all three more abstract, more vaporous, and thereby tying them firmly into Petrarch's highly controlled universe of meaning.

Although such virtuoso play upon an abstract vocabulary—all to create an insulated, specifically Petrarchan imaginative world—does bring the lady Laura to the reader's attention, the method is indirect, to say the least. The figure Laura which, as Umberto Bosco remarked long ago,[29] serves to concretize all the emotions expressed in the *Rime sparse*, remains throughout an oddly absent presence. Despite her apparent thematic importance as object of the poet's love and motive of his poetry, her actual name (as opposed to its paronomastic variations) appears but a few times within the entire collection, denying her all but the most tenuous linguistic existence. Nor is she ever clearly described. By the end of the *Rime sparse*, the reader knows little more than at the start: the loved one has blond hair, black eyes, and is somehow an "ideal" of beauty.

If we ask how Petrarch builds the apparently pervasive presence of Laura upon her virtual absence as a linguistic and realistically imaginable being, we begin to discover some of the thematic uses of Petrarch's lyric metonymy. For in the figure Laura—Petrarch's difficult to define, always unattainable object of love—and in the poet-lover's attitude toward her, the semantic effects most closely associated with the metonymic come strongly into play. Displacement, for instance, with its transference of thought or feeling along a chain of contiguous associations,[30] characterizes Petrarch's frequent descriptions of his loved one. In fact, his poems praising Laura tend to pass immediately beyond description to associated meditations on nature and myth that tell more in the end about the poet than the lady. And what do they bring sharply into focus? The poet's desire—that sense of lack, yearning, and incompletion that might well be considered the troubled, changeful source of nearly all Petrarch's poetry.[31]

For instance, a reading of the *Rime sparse* soon reveals how very deftly Petrarch has molded his lyric heritage to exaggerate the courtly and, later, stilnovistic theme of a poet-lover's desire for a forever distant, unreachable beloved. Petrarch's persona almost never addresses Laura directly, much less engages her in an imagined dialogue that would lend her a more palpable presence. If she speaks (and this is extremely rare), it is only when displaced into the totally inner world of the lover's own dreams, imagination, or visions. Far more often, the text remains purely monologic. And the single voice, praising the lady or reflecting on her powers, makes no attempt at realism or drama. If anything, its reliance on synecdoche and metonymy displaces Laura's imaginative presence (which could have been awakened by a second person "you") into a series of third person signs, a zone of things and thoughts that the linguist Benveniste appropriately calls the place of the "non-personne."[32] The poetic results of this apparently simple process of making a person or "you" into a thing or "it," are worth underscoring. For one, the poetic voice gains in poetic range, for it can now extend to every "thing" Laura becomes or suggests, while retaining its stance as courtly lover. At the same time, this voice can more firmly assert itself. It is, after all, now the only "person" of the text.

Rather than make Laura a lively human image, one that would add dramatic urgency to his monologues, the poet thus fragments her (according to the tradition of the medieval blazon) into bodily parts—the hand, eye, breast, hair, etc. Unattainable as an integral human presence in sonnets such as "I begli occhi ond' i' fui percosso" (sonnet 75) and "O bella man, che mi destringi 'l cor," (sonnet 199), Laura—or rather the physical objects into which she has been fragmented—passes into a distant, if erotically charged plane of words, all artistically molded, all ultimately referring (even, as here, in their very first lines), more to the speaker's than to Laura's experience.

Petrarch effects other fruitful modes of indirection, such as the classically metonymic movement from person (in this case Laura) to her setting. Instead of naming Laura, or trying to represent her, the persona simply praises what is next to, contiguous to, her being. The most frequent indirection of this sort alludes to Laura through the natural world.[33] Though an excellent example is doubtless canzone 126, "Chiare, fresche et dolci acque," the technique does color Petrarch's sonnets as well. Laura's walks in nature, for instance, occasion hyperbolic quatrains such as these:

> Lieti fiori et felici, et ben nate herbe
> che madonna pensando premer sòle;
> piaggia ch'ascolti sue dolci parole
> et del bel piede alcun vestigio serbe;
>
> schietti arboscelli et verdi frondi acerbe,
> amorosette et pallide vïole;
> ombrose selve, ove percote il sole
> che vi fa co' suoi raggi alte et superbe;
> (sonnet 162)

And, since constant association has made the natural world her sign, she can remain an equally potent force even after her death, as the opening of sonnet 320 clearly indicates:

> Sento l'aura mia anticha, e i dolci colli
> veggio apparire, onde 'l bel lume nacque
> che tenne gli occhi mei mentr'al ciel piacque
> bramosi et lieti, or li tèn tristi et molli.
>
> O caduche speranze, o penser' folli!
> Vedove l'erbe et torbide son l'acque
> et vòto et freddo 'l nido in ch'ella giacque,
> nel qual io vivo, et morto giacer volli,

As might be expected in Petrarch's complex rhetoric, metaphors drawn from the natural world also contribute to Laura's image. But generally, such metaphors serve the governing powers of displacement. Here, for instance, they disperse her "self" into even more de-personalized synecdochic "parts":

> Onde tolse Amor l'oro, et di qual vena,
> per far due treccie bionde? e 'n quali spine
> colse le rose, e'n qual piaggia le brine
> tenere et fresche, et die' lor polso et lena?
> (sonnet 220)

But it is through the metonymic displacement of Laura the woman into the mythic narrative of Daphne and Apollo that Petrarch offers his most original, and most poetically fruitful allusions. Associating Laura with the mythic Daphne/laurel, the object of love can at one and the same time be displaced and transformed into the figure of the similarly unreachable, desired Daphne; she can be sought by the poet and, on another level, reappropriated by him as confirmation of his desired artistic immortality. Thus, we find Laura in the mythic guise of Daphne in sonnets such as "Il figliuol di Latona avea già nove" (43) or here, in 34:

> Apollo, s'anchor vive il bel desio
> che t'infiammava a le thesaliche onde,

> et se non ài l'amate chiome bionde,
> volgendo gli anni, già poste in oblio:

Such mythic displacement also crowns the persona's reflection on his quest for poetic eternity in this well-known passage from canzone 30, "Giovene donna sotto un verde lauro." Here, the implications of displacement, desire, and poetic immortality join powerfully through the well-built mythic associations, "Laura"/ "lauro":

> I' temo di cangiar pria volto et chiome
> che con vera pietà mi mostri gli occhi
> l'idolo mio, scolpito in vivo lauro:
> che s'al contar non erro, oggi à sett'anni
> che sospirando vo di riva in riva
> la notte e'l giorno, al caldo ed a la neve.
>
> Dentro pur foco, et for candida neve,
> sol con questi pensier', con altre chiome,
> sempre piagendo andrò per ogni riva,
> per far forse pietà venir negli occhi
> di tal che nascerà dopo mill'anni,
> se tanto viver pò ben colto lauro.

In ways such as these, the reification or, better, the textualization of Laura reaches unusually cosmic proportions. So clearly does she become a figment of language that the reader today is tempted to ask the same question as Petrarch's own contemporaries: Is Laura only a name chosen for its homonomy with what seems to matter most to Petrarch, the poetic crown of laurels? It is, of course, even harder to answer this question today than in the fourteenth century, though we can still read Petrarch's words of protest.[34] What we do know from the *Rime sparse* is that if Laura serves as the apparent focal point of Petrarch's ruminations, his refusal to personalize her, transforming her instead into a series of self-reflexive objects, seems but a device to help lend the poet his own poetic identity. The semantic effects of "Laura" / "lauro" / "l'aura" / "l'aureo" are no less mirroring reflections than the sounds themselves. And what they mirror is ultimately the desiring poet-

The Petrarchan Sonnet / 29

speaker, fully reflected in his extensive play of words. They rightly suggest that the sexual other of the *Rime sparse* acts as little more than a means to present more clearly the image of the speaking self, the same.

As the lover of a textualized Laura, the Petrarchan voice remains, then, the single, if infinitely complex person of the sequence, its only real linguistic and thematic subject. Reflecting this lyric center as an earlier world mirrored its creator, Petrarch's poetic universe grows emphatically anthropocentric, with the figure of the poet controlling its most distant reaches. Of this effect, even the poem of praise, "L'aura che 'l verde lauro," is an excellent example.

Like most of Petrarch's sonnets, this too proceeds logically enough, tracing a cause-effect pattern of thought that takes the poet from apparent contemplation of Laura to rapt introspection. Beginning with an echo of Laura's name and a synecdochic reference to her golden hair, the poem soon exalts her as nature's most perfect creation, the "candida rosa." Then, with the increasingly explicit presence of the poetic voice at the sonnet turn, comes the poet's fear of Laura's death—a fear for the world's sake, and for his own: "O vivo Giove, / manda, prego, il mio in prima che 'l suo fine." But if the "candida rosa," metamorphosed now into the "sole" of the world and the "luce" of the poet's eyes, appears to be the poem's source of life, Petrarch's mounting references to the governing voice—"il mio . . . fine," "io," "li occhi miei," "l'alma," "l'orecchie,"—loudly proclaim otherwise. It is rather the poet, with his love, his fears, and his anaphoric phrases, who attracts and centers the reader's attention. We follow the imaginings of the speaker's inner world. "Laura," displaced as usual into the distant reaches of nature's ideal, merely lends visibility to his personally painful but poetically powerful introspection.

Rarely named, never confronted, seldom present as a "you," Laura by her very absence tells the real story of the *Rime sparse*: the story of the poet speaker and his often unhappy, unending desires. Of course, whenever we consider a range of lyrics in the collection, it quickly becomes evident that they gain their fascination because they tell of far more than a simply stated desire for a woman. Thanks to Petrarch's well-orchestrated universe of words, Laura's displacement results in an unusual poetic richness. Though the poet's quest may begin with "Laura," it does not end there. "Laura" is but the condition of possibility that allows the poet speaker to develop his quest for self, be this defined in terms of fame, eternity, understanding, or simply, peace.

RHETORICAL VOICE

That a quest for selfhood is central to the *Rime sparse* is clear from its first, rhetorically vivid, poem:

> Voi ch'ascoltate in rime sparse il suono
> di quei sospiri ond'io nudriva 'l core
> in sul mio primo giovenile errore
> quand'era in parte altr'uom da quel ch'i' sono,
>
> del vario stile in chi'io piango et ragiono
> fra le vane speranze e'l van dolore,
> ove sia chi per prova intenda amore
> spero trovar pietà, non che perdono.
>
> Ma ben veggio or sí come al popol tutto
> favola fui gran tempo, onde sovente
> di me medesmo meco mi vergogno;
>
> et del mio vaneggiar vergogna è 'l frutto,
> e 'l pentersi, e 'l conoscer chiaramente
> che quanto piace al mondo è breve sogno.

As it introduces the *Rime sparse*, this retrospective sonnet seems to gesture toward a basic change in the poet's perspective, perhaps even a conversion, that we would expect to play itself out in the poems to follow. Yet a reading of the entire collection, including the final canzone to the Virgin, reveals that the poet does not, at least in the limits of the *Rime sparse*, achieve divine peace. As Robert Durling puts it, the collection culminates at most in a prayer for help.[35]

Upon closer examination, we see that Petrarch's characteristic emphasis upon style, rhetoric, and especially, a turn to a grammatically dominating "io," modifies our reading of what appears to be a traditional palinode. "Voi ch'ascoltate" glorifies the poet and his craft as much as it deplores a lover's experience. By a careful choice of words, the poet marks the rift between art and life. He actually seems to delight in telling us that his poetry deals in purely verbal—and particularly well-wrought—coin. He offers his "rime" as a resonance or echo of sighs ("il suono" / "di quei sospiri ond'io nudriva 'l core") rather than sighs themselves. Only through the mediation of changing styles ("vario stile") can a poem present this poet's changing moods (his "vane speranze" and "van dolore"). By the end of the octave, grammar itself calls on the reader to pity the author's style as much as his style of life: "del vario stile in ch'io piango et ragiono . . . spero trovar pietà, non che perdono."

Our awareness of poetic artfulness only grows through Petrarch's phonic effects. Alliteration and assonance draw out the poem's linear, musical dimensions. Reaching a crescendo in the sestet, alliterative patterns such as "favola fui" (line 10), "me medesmo meco mi vergogno" (line 11), "vaneggiar vergogna" (line 12) and "conoscer chiaramente" (line 13) subside into the assonantal e's of lines 14–16. But, as in "Solo e pensoso," nothing puts Petrarch's self-conscious artistry before the reader more eloquently than the poem's elaborate, tightly controlled, grammatical figures. And of these syntactical variations—including a series of interrupting clauses, verbal repetitions, and a parade of syntactic couplings—the one most likely both to catch the reader's eye and bring it the image of a governing voice is the dramatic grammatical inaccuracy (or anacoluthon) that determines the path of the first long, meandering sentence. The poem opens with a direct address to the reader ("Voi"), while words keyed to sound—"ascoltate," "suono," "rime"—project the quatrain's public nature. But just before the sonnet's formal turn, grammar itself takes a surprising turn away from the reader and toward a meditation self-centering in grammar and theme. What appears in lines 1–7 to be a repentant communication here becomes an artistically self-conscious monologue that emphatically focuses on the "io," excluding the reader from any role but that of sympathetic listener and observer.

Proceeding in its new, more private voice, the sestet undermines all illusions of self-abnegating confession. What sort of shame does it finally describe? One that comes from a public display of love and ends by publishing a chain of rhetorically perfect assonantal synonyms of self: "di me medesmo meco mi vergogno." What is the final fruit of the poet's youthful "vaneggiar"? Shame, yes. Repentance, yes. But above all, a knowledge of earthly transience conveyed in a line that rings less with distaste than with keen poetic nostalgia: "'l conoscer chiaramente / che quanto piace al mondo è breve sogno."

Such a nostalgic and self-referential proem can hardly be read as an altogether traditional expression of *contemptu mundi*. It is at least as much a bittersweet memorial to the pleasures and pains of earthly experience, whose grammatical turn to monologue only highlights the role of an insistently self-dramatizing poet.

Although the mode of self-assertion evident here is so frequent in the *Rime sparse* as to be almost typical, the grammatical hegemony of the poetic voice can exert itself in other ways as well. For instance, Petrarch occasionally allows his sonnets to develop through more repetitive structures, choosing analogical figures, and paying more attention to referential imagery and associative space. But even in sonnets such as 134, "Pace non trovo," which we might take as an instructive exception to Petrarch's usual mode, the "io" fully dominates the poem's other images.

> Pace non trovo, et non ò da far guerra;
> e temo, et spero; et ardo, et son un ghiaccio;
> et volo sopra 'l cielo et giaccio in terra;
> et nulla stringo, et tutto 'l mondo abbraccio.
>
> Tal m'à in pregion, che non m'apre né serra,
> né per suo mi riten né scioglie il laccio;
> et non m'ancide Amore, et non mi sferra,
> né mi vuol vivo, né mi trae d'impaccio.

> Veggio senza occhi, et non ò lingua et grido;
> et bramo di perir, et cheggio aita;
> et ò in odio me stesso, et amo altrui.
>
> Pascomi di dolor, piangendo rido;
> egualmente mi spiace morte et vita:
> in questo stato son, donna, per voi.

Here, Laura is unreachable and, from the poet-speaker's perspective, must remain so. Passions are never fulfilled nor, given the tradition as Petrarch used it, do they end. In the course of the sonnet's four paratactic sentences, the figure antithesis constructs an almost mimetic pattern of language. For its semantic oppositions erect figurative "walls" at the sonnet's edge that enclose the meaning of each phrase. In this sonnet, where antitheses develop over the course of the verse or hemistich, the walls are buttressed by the pause and graphic space surrounding each line. The poet's situation of impossible but enduring love thus comes to the reader in the nearest rhetorical equivalent of a prison, fortified by repetitions of virtually the same figure for thirteen lines, and thematically present in stanza two.

"Pace non trovo" derives its self-reflexive impact largely from the referential space on which these antitheses draw. In fact, whatever thematic change occurs here—and there is not very much to be sure—is neither temporal nor particularly logical in character, but spatial: namely, a projection and gradual restriction of the speaking persona. Upon close observation, the effect seems to arise primarily because the antitheses organize other, smaller rhetorical figures that serve to expand the poem's cognitive dimension. Through a variety of tropes—metonymy, synecdoche, but especially hyperbole and metaphor—an outside world of images does, so to speak, enter the lyric chamber.

But as we might expect, Petrarch's syntax does not allow this imagery to build a world of its own. Instead, the lyric voice systematically impinges upon each trope until it exchanges its ordinary powers of outward reference for controlled self-reflection. If "pace" and "guerra," for instance, might alone conjure antithetical images, "io" manages to upstage both, taking grammatical and semantic charge with "non trovo" and "non ò." In this way, through the relentless intrusion of a lyric voice, ordinarily impersonal substantives and the tropes they build acquire a characteristically subjective feel.

This is not to say that Petrarch's referential images lack poetic effect. In fact, such figures succeed in this sonnet, much as they do in "Solo e pensoso," in amplifying the poetic self, making its inner world more perceptible. Metaphor concretizes abstract emotion, for instance, in order to strike the hyperbolic antithesis "ardo, et son un ghiaccio," while self-anatomizing synecdoches mass in tercet one and the beginning of tercet two to support the larger figure antithesis, "Veggio senza occhi, et non ò lingua et grido." A powerful and, in the *Rime sparse*, rather frequent "psychological" synecdoche transforms poet into both subject and object: "ò in odio me stesso." The figure of tercet two, "pascomi di dolor," is complex, both a synecdoche of emotion and a concretizing metaphor. In the second quatrain, between these clusters of metaphor and synecdoche, metonymy reigns and with it the ultimate thematization of the poet's prison of love. Here, the poet-speaker assumes a new grammatical posture, object rather than subject. But since "Amore," the nominal subject, is itself but a clear metaphoric projection of the imprisoned self, the trope turns inward precisely at the sonnet turn for the Petrarchan sonnet's familiar "inner scene."

At first subject of the world without, then restricted as imprisoned object of his own emotion, at last viewing with agonizing detachment the lyric self and masochistically feeding upon it, the speaker redirects meaning only in the sonnet's last two lines. Distancing the whole through a third person summary, he writes: "in questo stato son, donna, per voi."

Such self-centering techniques, as they play themselves out with variation in the grammar of single sonnet structures, permit some more general conclusions about Petrarch's style and meaning. For as the poems we have so far examined suggest, his rhetorical preferences are of a somewhat different nature than those of our day or even those of many poets of the fourteenth century. Though Aristotelian rhetoric, still preeminent in Petrarch's time, might prize tropes and particularly metaphors for their cognitive effects[36]—their ability to replace the usual and proper expression with an unusual but even more truthful and more lively substitute—the fact remains that Petrarch's poetry is seldom remarkable for this alone. As we have seen, metaphoric tropes do have their place within the *Rime sparse*. But theirs might best be described as a strong supporting role. A deft manipulation of lexicon and grammar makes almost every figure, trope as well as grammatical scheme, gain authority not from what seems to stand outside the poet, in the image-filled referential world to which metaphoric language ordinarily points, but from what appears within, that flexible and changing voice presented as the source of each lyric performance.

For this reason alone, Petrarch's poetics should probably be visualized differently than most. Rather than view his tropes according to the traditional hierarchy, in which metaphor stands at the top as the most genial expression by analogy of a proper statement, Petrarch's figures and tropes would better be arranged according to their metonymic or performative emphasis, on a linear axis figuring the syntagmatic. One might thus begin with the larger, more important, grammatical units, then the smaller designs, then the tropes that change meaning with a lesser dependence on syntagmatic play, until at last emphasis shifts to that realm of associations, the paradigmatic, where metaphor appears.

hyper-baton,	anas-trophe,	antith-esis,	reification, personifi-cation,	metonymy,	synecdoche,	replacement metaphor
Visible syntagm			dependence on			Invisible paradigm

If this scheme has the advantage of representing Petrarch's poetics as one that resists the traditional dominance of metaphor, it also goes some way to revealing the starring role played by the dramatized first person voice. In a syntactically powerful idiom such as Petrarch's, with the reduced impact it lends to metaphoric tropes, the cognitive reach of language bows to the performative, the rhetorically persuasive. What we imagine above all is the voice we hold responsible for each complex syntactic unit.

This rhetorical emphasis has, moreover, some historically relevant corollaries. In Petrarch's poetics, the cognitive reach of language so typical of medieval allegory—and we think at once of Petrarch's precursor, Dante—is rejected for a more textually immanent, more horizontal process of meaning that draws every other sense firmly into the poet's own distinctive drive for meaning and for self.

Such a historically ground-breaking mode was doubtless a conscious effort on Petrarch's part—one spurred not only by an understandable "anxiety of influence," great though that must have been as he looked back on Dante's achievement, but also by his scorn for the world in which he lived and his fascination with the classical past.[37] He read the Roman poets more than those of his own day. And in these works, he discovered—and clearly imitated—a self completely unabashed at its poetic prominence. He also rejected the metaphysically oriented scholasticism still in vogue in his day and, insisting on a strictly human viewpoint,[38] (a mere mortal, he thought, can aspire to no more) he described himself as a "moral philosopher and a poet." In a manner wholly consistent with the anthropocentric focus of his poetics and his own restless search for spiritual stability, Petrarch turned to questions of the will, to ethics, and to rhetoric in its Latinate, Ciceronian, sense.[39] In this perspective, rhetoric is not a mere series of ornamental figures subsumed to higher philosophical meanings. Rhetoric, in the broad sense in which Petrarch understood it, carries philosophy within itself.

With such rhetorical—as opposed to metaphysical—priorities, it is not surprising that Petrarch places new value on intratextual coherence, unity, and form, the very qualities likely to attentuate a strict correspondence of language to any concrete or metaphysical truth. At the same time, and in a clearly classical vein, he privileges the human element over any external framework. This choice has enormous implications for the *Rime sparse*, which we have seen. It means that Petrarch's writing, including his poetry, would gain its significance not by referring to hierarchies of being outside it, but by the very coherence the performing poet could establish among its signs.

Such a rhetorical as opposed to metaphysical inspiration stands in the background as Petrarch carefully refines his words into what Freccero has aptly termed an "idolatrous" mode.[40] Compared to allegorical usage, Petrarch's signs defy any stable relationship to truths beyond them, and the medieval sense of time, whose end in an allegorical framework would be given in advance as the fulfillment of God's plan, is broken. What the poet produces instead is a poetry of discrete moments whose ultimate source and end are no more than a very human poetic voice, endlessly striving to come to grips with its significance.

Thus, the Petrarchan sonnet often questions its own project and leaves its statements semantically open, almost as if they could continue interminably were the sonnet not restricted in time and space by its very form. But in spite of what can only be considered an inevitable internal questioning, Petrarch's sonnets seldom neglect to place the image of a poetic self, however tormented, however self-doubting and self-analytical, at their imaginative center.

Still, it is important to emphasize that, contrary to a purely theoretical expectation,[41] Petrarch's inner voice, the imaginative focus of his grammatically visible or rhetorical emphasis, can never itself be reduced to a totalizing metaphor, an integral "being." In the context of Petrarch's writing, the speaking voice may strive for sovereignty, artistic prominence, and power. One could even say that it achieves this. But at the same time, this voice claims neither stability nor integrity. Its "essere" remains, as Thomas Greene has put it, "incerto."[42] In fact, it can only be imagined by the reader in terms of its continual displacements and transformations, its painful, metonymic becoming.

At least in part, this probably has to do with the transience that Petrarch perceived all around him, recorded, and attempted, as far as humanly possible, to defy. Critics have often noted that a fear of transience seems to haunt the *Rime sparse*.[43] But if we can judge by Petrarch's prose as well as his poetry, this is not a concern that a woman named Laura or any single human encounter taught him. Instead, it is apparently something endemic to the poetic personality. Petrarch tells us, for instance, that he recalls reading the classics as a young man—Horace, Juvenal, Vergil, Ovid, Seneca, Cicero—and noting less the grammatical lessons he was to derive from them than the ideas they expressed about life's transience: "I noted with sureness . . . the ideas themselves, the poverty of this miserable life, the brevity, the rapidity . . . the irrecuperabilty of time, the flowering of a transient and mutable life, the fleeting beauty of a rosy face, the unchecked flight of a youth that will never return and the deceit of a quietly creeping old age; finally, the wrinkles and the illnesses and the unhappiness and pain and the harsh implacable inclemency of indomitable death."[44] In the *De Remediis* (I.1), he ties his stark awareness of time to the very syllables he writes: "Now, with each stroke of the syllables I write, some part of my life passes away."[45]

Still, if Laura did not teach Petrarch these hard lessons, she and the poetic laurel clearly offer means to express them. "La vita fugge e non s'arresta una hora," he writes in sonnet 272 and, in sonnet 195, "Di dí in dí vo cangiando il viso e 'l pelo." Even earlier in the *Rime sparse*, sonnets such as 32, "Quanto più m'avicino al giorno extremo" and 101, "Lasso, ben so che dolorose prede," painfully portray the poet's awareness of the inevitable end of beauty—and of life itself.

Unfortunately for Petrarch's hope for spiritual peace, his keen awareness of human temporality does not initiate a movement toward transcendence. Doubtless this is partly because he detects time's changefulness nowhere more clearly than in his own internal vacillations: "Sentio inexpletum quoddam in praecordiis meis semper," ("I feel within me something unsatisfied, always"), writes Petrarch in the *Secretum*.[46] As Calcaterra mentions and Bosco agrees, here is the very crux of Petrarch's poetic vacillations, uncertainties, and the desire that seems to drive him.[47]

Since Petrarch can see no end to his desires, he might at least hope to channel them properly—that is, toward God. But this, too, seems an impossibility. Augustinus warns Franciscus in the *Secretum*, for instance, that he sins above all by not subsuming his love of an earthly creature to his love of the Creator. But Franciscus confesses he can do nothing about it.[48] Indeed, even Petrarch's dreams of eternal heavenly peace seem to entail little more than an earthliness perfected and purified of transience, as he suggests both in the *Trionfo dell-Eternità*, and here in this particularly forthright discussion in the *Seniles* (III.9):

> Oh celestial life, always happy and always the same, that knows neither past nor future: all is present. Whatever pleased once, always pleases and always will please, immutable and eternal, since it soothes but does not diminish the desire under which one labors, satisfies it but does not extinguish it, cools it in order to inflame it; and in short, satiety does not insinuate itself and never can, nor does one fear its end or its change.[49]

The image of the Virgin herself, crowning the final moments of the *Rime sparse*, seems to be merely a dream of earthly perfection, more an eternalized Laura than a divine being.

In such a quandary—between the impossibility of Christian transcendence on the one hand, and dreams of earthly eternity on the other—poetry might well seem to offer the most a mere human could hope of peace and eternity. Here, indeed, external transience might gain some stability in the limited eternity of verbal form. And here, a poetic persona might at least appear to govern the metamorphoses of desire through a careful molding of language. To create such a voice, endowed with a distinctly musical, well-wrought, memorable style, is a small earthly miracle. To lend it self-reflexive power within its own universe of words is to set into relief a thoroughly human and, in the fourteenth century, a thoroughly revolutionary, classically inspired quest.

The word *quest* deserves underscoring. Without tying selfhood to expected truths and safe models, Petrarch's persona is bound to be problematic. Even more so when we recall that language is its only medium. As Petrarch (and Augustine) well knew, language inevitably impedes desire's unequivocal expression.[50] Its limitations themselves end, as several recent critics have noted, by putting the integrity of a self into question.[51] The famous canzone of the metamorphoses, "Nel dolce tempo de la prima etade" (23), that transforms the poet from lover to laurel to stone and beyond, most explicitly expresses this uncertainty. But even the motivated symbolism of the Petrarchan lexicon can be disturbing. Applying a single sign interchangeably to more than one persona of the lyric collection produces ambiguity as well as an intensely limited inner world. And although the poet binds up these various ambiguities through the force of his grammar, with its creation of a voice and the strong presence of an "io," his complex grammar that so effectively dramatizes this self in fact remains riddled with questioning.

But in his pervasive self-questionings—be they overtly thematic or subtly grammatical—Petrarch's revolutionary quest for an earthly, yet immortalized self is not so much undermined as deepened and dramatized. In fact, Petrarch's self-reflexive poetics might be said to achieve its greatest profundity precisely in its presentation of the inevitable uncertainties that occupy any serious meditation on spirit and emotion and any attempt to describe them.

THE POETIC QUEST AND THE SONNET MYTH

The reader's ability to imagine Petrarch's poetic quest for self grows through more than the manipulation of language in individual sonnets. It builds, too, through the poet's careful arrangement of texts within the *Rime sparse* as a whole. The collection breeds a special sort of interplay among its 366 poems. Along with the repetition of words and imagery, chronology and sequence help construct the fiction of a poetic diary. Literary scholarship has provided us with the dates of composition for individual poems. We also possess earlier versions of the collection, in which the lyrics are placed differently. All of this only underscores the deliberateness of the final organization, with its spare chronology of events—the *innamoramento*, or falling in love, the absences and illnesses, Laura's death, the poet's anguish, and prayers for peace. Throughout, as stalwart markers, anniversary poems commemorate the passing years of the poet's love.[52] Even the space left in the manuscript, separating those poems supposedly written in Laura's lifetime from those written after, artfully reinforces the impression of autobiography.

If Petrarch's *Rime sparse* resembles a diary in this temporal punctuation, it also resembles it in the brevity of its entries, each with its slightly different, yet recognizably Petrarchan *ragionar*. Hopes, fears, frustrations, expectations, losses—all juxtaposed and presented one after another—shape the inner, subjective world of a persona. Within this web of words and their mirroring meanings, an "io" steps forward, striving to distill whatever substance, whatever truth about its human state that human transience permits—and striving also to eternalize this difficult quest in poetry.

Thus, Petrarch does not hesitate to juxtapose a sonnet such as 61, "Benedetto sia 'l giorno," exalting love and glory, with 62, "Padre del ciel," an invocation to God in which the poet, now in the eleventh year of his love, regrets time spent in the desire of love rather than in Christian repentance. Nor does he refrain from expressing intense sorrow at Laura's death in a sonnet such as 305, "Anima bella da quel nodo sciolta," and, immediately after, in 306, "Quel sol che mi mostrava il camin destro," the spiritual lesson he knows he should derive from Laura's passing. Such variations would certainly cause confusion were we looking for development in the usual sense of the word. No story progresses through these poems. If anything, they accentuate the incompletion of the poet's attempt at self-definition. But what does progress is our ability to fictionalize the subjective voice, this voice never complete and at rest, but always striving, always becoming.

Events are rare in such continual introspection. And these few are caught in an intricate web of subjective meditation. The *innamoramento* is, of course, one of the major happenings of the *Rime sparse*, and the poet returns to it incessantly, lending it new meanings in relation to himself and his current state of mind. Thus we find remembrances of it at various points in the collection. Sonnet 90, "Erano i capei," is a particularly well-crafted one:

> Erano i capei d'oro a l'aura sparsi
> che 'n mille dolci nodi gli avolgea,

> e 'l vago lume oltra misura ardea
> di quei begli occhi, ch'or ne son sí scarsi;
>
> e 'l viso di pietosi color' farsi,
> non so se vero o falso, mi parea:
> i' che l'esca amorosa al petto avea,
> qual meraviglia se di subito arsi?
>
> Non era l'andar suo cosa mortale,
> ma d'angelica forma; et le parole
> sonavan altro, che pur voce humana.
>
> Uno spirito celeste, un vivo sole
> fu quel ch'i' vidi: et se non fosse or tale,
> piagha per allentar d'arco non sana.

On one level, we note here the same foregrounding of the poetic persona as we have seen in other sonnets. Words once more take on a smooth, musical quality—this time through assonance (in the *a*'s and *e*'s of quatrain one, for instance) and an enjambement of lines that ties the reader to the metonymic, beginning-to-end dimension of the text. And again, address to another is muted, to present instead a musicalized monologue.

Word choice and grammar delicately poise past and present, original scene and act of remembrance. The imperfect tense does double duty, conjuring the poet's time of reflection as well as the moment remembered. And as the sonnet paints Laura's youthful beauty, deictics and first person references cluster, especially in the second and fourth stanzas, reminding us that the vision originates in the poet's perception. In fact, such grammatical signals trace a redoubled turn to the self. If stanzas one and three recall Laura's beauty, stanzas two and four focus on the memorializing voice.

As we have come to expect, the poem's carefully balanced performative, grammatical dimension highlights more than just the subjective source; it also projects the speaker's metamorphic power. With the turn in line 8 and the rhetorical, self-justifying question ("i' che l'esca amorosa al petto avea, / qual meraviglia se di subito arsi?"), grammar repeats itself as it escalates the metaphoric praise. Described in nature in stanza one, Laura grows through the voice of the sonnet turn into "uno spirito celeste" and the familiar "vivo sole." But what finally attracts attention is not so much the beauty remembered as the poetic voice remembering.

It is a voice all the more vivid here for its ability to use another from the past to counterpoint its own lyric expression. In line 1 and again in lines 9–11, Petrarch alludes to Vergil who, in Book 1 of the *Aeneid*, tells of Aeneas's encounter with Venus, and his eventual recognition of her. But the poet dramatically undermines and transforms the sense of the original in the very course of drawing our attention to it. For as Thomas Greene notes, if the *Aeneid* presents a recognition of divinity in fine epic style, the sonnet voice, exploring as it does the uncertain field of subjective memory (more common to lyric than epic form) rends the perception of Laura's divinity with a host of typically Petrarchan hesitations: "Parea," he writes when describing the vision and adds even more pointedly, "Non so se vero o falso."[53] By such means, what might stand as a rival poetic voice becomes merely a foil for the very un-Vergilian vacillations of a more modern poet-lover. Petrarch's reach for a dimension of history perceived as so separate as to require what Thomas Greene calls a "metaphoric" resuscitation, characterizes an essential part of Petrarch's humanistic force.[54] But what is equally interesting—and equally indicative of his historical place—is that he has woven this metaphoric dimension, like his other, more time-limited metaphoric tropes, into his own self-defining discourse. Not only has he called upon this voice from the classical past; he has tamed its power, made it part of his own story, as melody uses harmony to intensify its line. Vergil does not offer transcendence beyond the poet's human state of vacillation and uncertainty, merely the means to delineate Petrarch's linear, grammatically heightened "performance" more fully.

Though examples of Petrarch's self-dramatizing rhetoric are seemingly endless, they highlight a poet who has refused to define his persona according to any precursor, classical or medieval, or any available system of philology or theology. He has refused to present it in terms of any given state or emotion. Rather, he has chosen to define it as process, changefulness, perennial self-questioning, perpetual quest—and has done so through the medium of rhetorically effective words molded, most often, in sonnet form. One wonders, in fact, whether Petrarch did not choose the sonnet as frequently as he did precisely for its ability to focus the quest for an earthly yet eternal self, and to do so in part through the poem's formal structure. Within its short scope, the sonnet effectively sets forth the poet's metonymic, grammatical patterning. It underscores the semantic dimensions of the metonymic, as meaning progresses—usually through argument or narrative—from beginning to end of the poem.

Most of the sonnets of the *Rime sparse*, like those we have considered in the preceding pages, shape a distinct semantic metamorphosis between their first and last lines. Such sonnet transformations may take the shape of a single striking analogy, or several variations on a given theme. But far more frequently, they develop their themes as logical or rhetorical arguments governed by the strong poetic voice. The forward movement of Petrarch's poetic rationalizations, such as we have seen in "Solo e pensoso," "Voi ch'ascoltate," "Erano i capei," and "L'aura che 'l verde lauro," go some way to undermining the sonnet's otherwise repetitive form, by drawing the reader's attention away from the closure of end-rhymes toward the more differential process of syntax and *ragionamento*. So involved does the reader become in following the reasoning of the poetic argument that some more traditional aspects of the sonnet may be momentarily eclipsed. But what Petrarch almost never subverts is the Italian sonnet's most distinctive and, in his hands, most self-reflexive feature, the turn from octave to sestet.

If the sonnet originally used changes in thought and rhyme to signal a transition around line 8, Petrarch greatly heightened this formal potential through his own effective use of style and meaning. Most often, two changes occur here. For one, a metonymic discourse frequently gives way to a more metaphoric, more cognitively rich, expression. But even more important, the sonnet turn highlights the voice of the persona. For though a lyric voice pervades the entire lexicon and syntax, variations in textual subjectivity help shape each poem. A qualitatively different sonnet middle, characterized by a more dramatic first person voice, generally marks the turn from octave to sestet, and becomes the imaginative ground for the more metaphoric and often more clearly subjective statements that follow.

Sometimes, the change in lyric presence comes with a rush, as in the sudden appearance of the (grammatically unnecessary) subject pronoun "io" at the turn of "Solo e pensoso." Although other references to the lyric self appear earlier in the poem, none compares with the suddenly active role the speaker takes here, at lines 8 and 9, as he prepares the reader for the more subjectively defined imagery that follows. But a dramatization of the lyric voice may be much more subtle as well, arising through variations in grammatical persons of the verb, through changes in tense (with the *passato prossimo*, future and present revealing most clearly the speaker's temporal perspective), through intensified temporal and spatial moorings such as "qui" and "ora," through demonstratives, or even through subjective remarks, intruding upon more purely referential statements to offer a subjective insight or refer the reader to an "inner" world.

In "Voi ch'ascoltate," for instance, language most clearly depicts the subjective presence in line 9, with its strong first person statement, "veggio or sí," followed by the self-dramatizing reflections at the end of the tercet: "di me medesmo meco mi vergogno." Though the entire sonnet draws in the dimensions of the persona, this moment of the text brings grammar to its most subjective pitch and prepares us for the meditations that close the text. "Erano i capei" takes a metamorphosing inward turn at the end of the octave, exactly where an indirect description of Laura gives way to the persona's self-justifying question: "i' che l'esca amorosa al petto avea, / qual meraviglia se di subito arsi?" Again, in "Pace non trovo," where the entire text seems introverted, in spite of its myriad tropes, the effect is most intense in tercet one, with its self-subjugating "ò in odio me stesso," where the voice is both subject and object. "L'aura che 'l verde lauro" clearly allows a concentration on the lyric self to mount in lines 7 and 9, turning here directly from third person description to an exclamation focusing on the self: "O vivo Giove, / manda, prego, il mio in prima che 'l suo fine." This self-referential focus continues in line 9 with its "sí chi'io non veggia." The rest of the sonnet's development of Laura's meaning for the poet depends upon this central introspective moment.

What is perhaps most remarkable, though, is the regularity with which Petrarch resorts to this quite literal linguistic self-centering, even when the sonnet seems far less apt to be a personalized statement than those we have so far examined. It is particularly curious to consider, as a final example, a sonnet such as 190, "Una candida cerva," that restates the "hunt of love," Petrarch's well-worked convention of lyric desire, in a distanced, dreamlike form more typical of myth:[55]

> Una candida cerva sopra l'erba
> verde m'apparve, con duo corna d'oro,
> fra due riviere, all'ombra d'un alloro,
> levando 'l sole a la stagione acerba.
>
> Era sua vista sí dolce superba
> ch'i' lasciai per seguirla ogni lavoro:
> come l'avaro che 'n cercar tesoro
> con diletto l'affanno disacerba.
>
> 'Nessun mi tocchi—al bel collo d'intorno
> scritto avea di diamanti et di topazi—:
> libera farmi al mio Cesare parve.'
>
> Et era 'l sol già vòlto al mezzo giorno,
> gli occhi miei stanchi di mirar, non sazi,
> quand'io caddi ne l'acqua, et ella sparve.

The poem, to be sure, reflects many of the same techniques we have seen elsewhere. It manages a large number of substantives referring to nature (presenting Laura, in fact, as the elusive "cerva,"), the supernatural (through references to "Caesar," a traditional metaphor for God) and, of course, to the poet himself.

The Petrarchan Sonnet / 47

But though the poem's symbolic web of language recalls any number of Petrarchan sonnets—and though the theme of the chase is central to Laura's displacement into myth—grammatical time and person distance this particular text to an unusual degree. Rather than invoking the present or imperfect, the distant past here dominates, with five of the sonnet's verbs in the historical past, two in the pluperfect, one in the imperfect, and only two in the present. Such a displacement of personal experience into a sequence of events occurring in the distant past moves the poem somewhat out of the usual domain of lyric poetry in a direction more typical of history or myth. The impression of myth grows through the almost total dependence on the grammatical third person, both in the verbs and in the numerous substantives that vastly outweigh references to the speaker himself.

But this sonnet-myth grows perhaps most powerfully through its three-part temporal development. First the deer appears at dawn ("levando 'l sole"), then the poet-lover begins his chase (described in quatrain two and tercet one), and finally the deer disappears and the lover "falls" at noon ("al mezzo giorno"). Compared to the barest mythic or folk sequence, which might be described as a "referential text through which an initial attribute or situation is transformed by a process of mediation into a different attribute or situation,"[56] "Una candida cerva" seems to lack nothing. The poet-persona's initial situation indeed changes in the course of the text, from a contemplation of the "cerva" at dawn to his mysterious fall at the end of the sonnet. Between the two occurs the mediating action of the chase.

Although "Una candida cerva" is unusual in its grammatical tense and extensive use of the third person, it is scarcely the only sonnet that, with its three-part sequence and mediating center, resembles myth. On the contrary, even the most seemingly immediate and lyric sonnets evoke this mythic structure, if only through their three-part enunciation. In such cases, the time in which events unfold is simply the beginning-to-end sequence of the persona's *ragionar*. Its mediating middle is the strong poetic voice at the center.

Even in this sonnet, referential though it is, a significant passage speaks directly of the narrator's feelings, and the moment occurs precisely with the sonnet's turn. Not only does the first grammatical subject pronoun appear in line 6 ("i' lasciai"), the comparison in lines 7 and 8 reflects directly upon the speaker's "inner world," his greedy, bittersweet pleasure in the chase. And, in a manner reminiscent of "Erano i capei," this pivotal moment effectively transforms the sonnet events from a natural to a supernatural plane, reminding us of the metamorphosing power of the poet. Although stanza one brims with the wonder of a sudden apparition ("m'apparve"), only stanza three projects the "cerva" onto a plane of communal legend and personal myth: " 'Nessun mi tocchi / . . . libera farmi al mio Cesare parve.' " The "cerva" takes on a more universal significance through the metaphorical reach to both the legend of Caesar's immortal deer and the Biblical "Noli me tangere" at the same time as it delineates more forcefully the persona's situation of unfulfilled desire. The chase goes on, but with a tone at once more personal and more universal.

Though I have suggested that this three-part sonnet movement, complemented here by an extreme referentiality and historical distance, lends the poem the shape of myth, it must be admitted that in its peculiarly lyric first person action, it remains something of its opposite. Myth traditionally mediates between two fixed and irreconcilable opposites. But the Petrarchan sonnet does not so much mediate between two fixed terms as generate one from the other in a passage through the sonnet's most lyric central portion. More than myth, the Petrarchan sonnet remains semantically open, open to the extent of the speaker's self-questioning desire.[57] It is only temporally closed. As such, the lyric center makes the Petrarchan sonnet a tiny emblem of human power and involvement in life's perplexing rhythm.

Looking forward to the sonnet's future and particularly to Petrarch's earliest imitators, one cannot help but note that lyric narratives of the sort present in "Una candida cerva," along with the poet's most visible rhetoric and most recurrent images, appear with extraordinary frequency. Yet one can hazard the guess that in the end it was Petrarch's particular build and structural centering of a very human voice in sonnet after sonnet—even more than his vast series of visible, translatable *topoi*—that captured the imagination of the Renaissance writers who followed and allowed both Petrarch and his sonnet to eventually achieve the earthly immortality he so passionately desired.

Chapter Two

Dramatic Metaphor
The Shakespearean Sonnet

> Farewell! thou art too dear for my possessing,
> And like enough thou know'st thy estimate,
> The charter of thy worth gives thee releasing;
> My bonds in thee are all determinate.
> For how do I hold thee but by thy granting,
> And for that riches where is my deserving?
> The cause of this fair gift in me is wanting,
> And so my patent back again is swerving.
> Thy self thou gav'st, thy own worth then not knowing,
> Or me to whom thou gav'st it, else mistaking,
> So thy great gift upon misprision growing,
> Comes home again, on better judgment making.
>   Thus have I had thee as a dream doth flatter,
>   In sleep a king, but waking no such matter.
>   —Sonnet 87[1]

"Farewell!" It is an exclamation that confronts the reader at the beginning of one of Shakespeare's most poignant sonnets. A first step in the poet's gradual illumination of image and form, this single word in the imperative mood immediately frames a dramatic moment in a human relationship: the poet-speaker's break with the fair young man who serves as the idealized love of the first 126 sonnets. Thanks largely to surrounding texts, reasons for this parting are not left altogether wanting. The placement of this sonnet in a small group of poems about a rival poet, and specifically after sonnet 86, which begins "Was it the proud full sail of his great verse," suggests that it is the speaker's loss of the young man's favor—as a patron, perhaps, as well as a friend—that prompts the poet's own farewell.

Dramatic situations such as this, that powerfully evoke concrete circumstances and the active speech of personae, have caused a good deal of speculation as to Shakespeare's actual relationship with the fair young man. John Dover Wilson writes, for instance, "After 86, a change inevitably takes place between Poet and Friend: Shakespeare has admitted that Chapman has a right to the favor the Friend shows him."[2] And Leishman, in a somewhat different vein, ponders the sixteenth-century relations between aristocrat and commoner: "That it was Shakespeare who had been made to feel like this rouses a disgust with aristocratic pretension which it requires remembrance of such a friend and patron as Beethoven's Archduke Rudolph to counterbalance."[3] But as the abundance of speculation and paucity of facts about Shakespeare's life suggest, any precise correspondence between Shakespeare the man and the sonnets he wrote is necessarily elusive.

What is no less interesting, and certainly more amenable to literary analysis, is the rhetorical strategy by which Shakespeare provokes a drama in the reader's mind—one with images lively enough, situations and persons particularized enough, to lend the appearance of historical situations, whether or not that is what they really are. Sonnet 87, for instance, requires the reader's imagination to conjure up most of the details of the dramatic farewell, guided generally by the surrounding sonnets, but more specifically by the poet's words as they shape the typical Shakespearean sonnet form of three quatrains and a couplet. Words whose ambiguity only begins to dissolve with the closing couplet, they convey a tone of sorrow crossed with bitterness.

From the very first line, grammar and semantics, the performative and more distinctly cognitive, seem to vie with one another, as they weave a network of contrary meanings joining the two protagonists. On the one hand, grammar maintains the usual courtly love hierarchy between lover and object. The syntactic core of the sentence—"thou art too dear"—prizes the subject "thou," as the prepositional phrase—"for my possessing"—makes plain that the lover's claims on the young man are limited, if not at an end. On the other hand, two more words—"dear" and "possessing" (both emphasized by the iambic pentameter stress)—present semantic ambiguities that strike the reader with a perplexing mixture of associations. "Dear" offers a choice between two distinct, if related, meanings: either "glorious, worthy, regarded with esteem and affection," when applied to a person, or "high-priced, costly, valuable," when referring to a thing.[4] The word "possessing" carries similar binary associations: either "sexual employment" with reference to a human being or, more commonly, "ownership, the holding of a thing or place." Coupled with "dear" and, like it, reflecting on the subject "thou," "possessing" colors its human subject with the unlikely suggestion of an inanimate thing.

If this slight shadow on the luster of "thou" scarcely undoes the conventional hierarchy between idealized object and poet-lover, it clearly lends the relationship new imaginative complexity. Moreover, since such semantic ambiguities begin in the text but resolve, to the extent they can, in the reader's mind, they make the reader, from line 1 onward, a virtual accomplice of the speaking self in what must be termed an act—not a mere description—of farewell. Throughout, the sonnet syntax works to set a dramatic scene, one that extends beyond poetic monologue to an encounter between an "I" and a "thou." At the same time, lexical ambiguities heighten the action, as they simultaneously attest to Shakespeare's artful handling of what might be called, in almost perfect contrast to Petrarch's rhetorical mode, an "invisible" sphere of verbal associations.

INVISIBLE RHETORIC

In the course of sonnet 87, syntactic patterns simulate a stiff legal argument, tailoring a logical train of thought to the close contours of fourteen end-stopped lines. At the same time, grammatical complications rise to a pitch of legalistic involution at quatrain three, as participial inversions testify to the climactic moment of the speaker's plea. But what strikes one most in this or virtually any Shakespearean sonnet, especially when compared to examples of Petrarch's verse, is not so much a metonymic chain with its "visible" grammar as a series of metaphoric "overlaps" of sense resolving in the space of the reader's mind.

The metaphoric dimension of language in which Shakespeare excels involves the reader in selecting and substituting linguistic elements at almost each point in the linear chain of words.[5] A poet who emphasizes this rhetorical dimension enlists the reader's mind in resolving a collision of semantically incompatible elements in the text. This inner resolution is precisely what generates metaphor's novel effects. A linguistic perspective such as this, proposed in Jakobson's essay on metaphor and metonymy, but also advanced with variations by countless others, is fully consonant with a distinctly modern perspective, one that has grown with the very texture of modern poetry. To use the phraseology of C. Day Lewis, modern poetics (and not simply that of a structuralist persuasion) finds "poetic truth struck out by the collision rather than the collusion of images."[6] A view like this, which makes poetry responsible for striking altogether new meanings and thus new truths, opposes the basically mimetic notion of metaphor that preceded.

Since Aristotle's claim that "metaphor is the transference of a name from the object to which it has a natural application,"[7] and until roughly the nineteenth century, metaphor was conceived largely within the framework of a representational view of art. Through its "improper" naming, metaphor provided a new verbal angle, a new insight into the referential world. If, in a quest for interpretation, the reader's mind might at times come to rest quite easily at metaphor's proper naming and, with it, the referential image that name elicits, at other times metaphor seemed to elude any adequate paraphrase, as though its meaning somehow transcended speech altogether. But regardless of the difficulty of assigning a specific and understandable meaning to metaphor, it was nonetheless considered a cognitive device, a means of telling the truth about the world with which every reader might be expected to be familiar—a truth even more essential than that which "proper" language, with its all too automatic meanings, normally permits.

Although it may no longer be tenable that metaphor—or much else for that matter—unveils a simple truth or hidden essence of life, it is clear to any reader of Shakespeare's poetry that his metaphorical imagery bears, at least in part, on a general, even a universal code of human experience. His images do not take the reader simply from life to a purer world of verbal creation. Instead, they invite new insights into the complexity of what we take to be life itself.

Thus, like any other metaphors written in any other time and place, Shakespeare's work through a juxtaposition of different lexical elements that spark new, previously uncoded concepts in the reader's mind. To this extent, Shakespeare's metaphors conform to Jakobson's twentieth-century description of the trope. But the Shakespearean sonnet prompts further explanation, for unlike a metaphoric poem by Mallarmé or William Carlos Williams, Shakespeare's does not radically redefine reference and reality. Although produced in the invisible space of the reader's associations, Shakespeare's metaphors do not so much install there a private world of the poet's own imagining as alter perceptions of easily recognizable objects and quite universal emotions. Shakespeare's sonnets, that is, seem to suggest that the semantic collision that we hold characteristic of any metaphor may well entail collusion as well—collusion with a store of broader containing references, references either so often repeated in the literary tradition or so frequently experienced in the larger text of life that they are quite generally accepted as human truths. Taking this more Nietzschean view of accepted truth as itself a sort of metaphoric repetition,[8] Shakespeare's metaphors indeed work, at least in part, mimetically. By pointing to, indeed overlapping with, codes of meaning established by literary and social convention, they imitate our conception of reality, if not perhaps its Aristotelian "essence."[9]

In this respect, Shakespeare's imagery is, on the one hand,

strikingly new, invariably unique, and, on the other hand, mimetic, partly repeating a larger, more generally accepted referential framework. Though Shakespeare probably never intended his sonnets for publication, but rather for the eyes of private friends, they are, in this rhetorical sense, among the most public sonnets ever written—open to the reader's experience, demanding his or her insight into a complex world that in many ways overlaps with the more ordinary, less intense world that is our own.

The metaphoric power of sonnet 87 comes, for instance, largely from lexical collisions that ultimately collude with at least two distinguishable public codes. One is what we might simply term the *realistic* framework of legal and social institutions. The second is Shakespeare's variation on an already conventional view of love. Words such as "estimate," "charter," "bonds," and "patent," derive from a strictly legal context, though they had appeared before in the Elizabethan sonnet. Through a series of artful collisions, Shakespeare elicits their hidden possibilities, questioning them and redefining them, producing in the end the metaphoric image of love as a legal exchange. Line 1 sets the pace for the sort of associative play that continues throughout. In the first quatrain, "charter," "bonds," and "determinate,"—by infecting more neutral words such as "possessing," "estimate," and "releasing,"—transform love into a matter of property rights. "Granting," "riches," and "patent," only reinforce the image in quatrain two, drawing with them more neutral terms like "hold," "cause," and "gift." In the third quatrain, "misprision" and "judgment" build up the legal metaphor, while "worth" and "gift," already associated with it, easily fall into line. Only the closing couplet takes a different tack. Exempting itself from the legal metaphor, just as a king in Shakespeare's day exempted himself from the common law,[10] it presents an alternative view of love—one more personalized, more direct and, as we shall see, ultimately more tragic.

The ambiguity that arises from the collisions of Shakespeare's legal diction has several important effects. For one, it demands of the reader a particularly intense participation, one that can be compared in its power not only to that demanded by the seventeeth-century lyrics of Donne and the so-called metaphysicals, but also by much later nineteenth and twentieth century texts. But as the sonnet asks us to resolve its meaning through a series of realistic legal references, it simultaneously urges us to reconsider our general expectations of the love sonnet and its courtly conventions. Rather than the usual private meditation on the effects of love or praise for the loved one, this sonnet, as we have seen, taps a societal, altogether worldly dimension in which contracts are made and broken, and courts of common law pass judgment in property cases. Shakespeare's inclusion of an altogether worldly dimension of meaning in a large number of sonnets is but one indication of the notable repetition-with-a-difference that marks his relationship to the sonnet tradition as it had developed from Petrarch's day to his own.

For the Renaissance poets who followed Petrarch (and the most important imitators waited more than a century to do their work of popularization and development), art typically entailed reproducing a prior model. To writers of the fifteenth and sixteenth centuries, Petrarch's sonnets, with their polished Latinate style building the image of a powerful, if struggling poetic self, became models of art and sometimes even of life, themselves deemed as worthy of imitation as the writings of Horace, Catullus, and Propertius. Indeed, Petrarch's sonnet form, his most distinctive themes, his phrases and his imagery, were often blindly repeated not only in Italy, but throughout Western Europe. It would not be an exaggeration to say that the sonnet as first popularized by Petrarch and his Italian imitators played a larger role than any other single form in building a highly competitive, if also cohesive, European literary community.

Not surprisingly, Italy responded first, initially adopting little more than Petrarch's sonnet form and his most apparent rhetoric.[11] But the fifteenth and sixteenth centuries, feeling the full effects of humanism as well as the rise of the new Platonic movement to which Petrarch's idealizing love lyric seemed to lend support, imitated his sonnets yet more faithfully. Authors such as Bembo, Della Casa, and Michelangelo exploit the Petrarchan tension between humanistic and metaphysical or religious concerns, as well as the more obvious love themes and figures.[12] With complex ideas to develop and a keen sense of poetic personality, these later poets prefer the sequence or collection to the individual sonnet.

Gradually, the sonnet tradition grew to be one of many signs of Italy's new cultural importance, closely associated with its historical role as heir to the classical past. Fed by the burgeoning wealth of the merchant cities of Florence, Rome, Venice, and Naples, Italy's was a general artistic dominance that other European courts eagerly emulated. On the continent and, somewhat later in England, the sonnet became a training ground for those who were consciously working to make illustrious their own vernacular tongues. To write a sonnet in France, England, Spain, or Germany during the sixteenth and early seventeenth centuries was to participate not only in a literary fashion, but in a political movement.

In the manifesto of the French Pléiade, the *Défense et illustration de la langue Française*, Du Bellay, for instance, urged poets, "sonne-moi ces beaux sonnets, non moins docte que plaisante invention italienne."[13] By imitating the Italian sonnet (and Du Bellay cites Petrarch's in particular), the French hoped to improve their own literary potential and eventually rival the Italians and even the classics themselves. In England, Puttenham would praise the early sonnet writers Wyatt and Surrey for cultivating the sophisticated Renaissance style he wanted his country to produce.[14] Writing a great sonnet or, better yet, a great sonnet sequence, helped establish, so it seemed, the strength of one's native vernacular and, simultaneously, one's national culture. In the period between Petrarch's *Rime sparse* and Shakespeare's *Sonnets*, the sonnet itself had become practically synonymous with good Renaissance poetic form, even high literature, one of the many signs of the rising nation-states in search of a more classical and therefore more universal patina.

Doubtless, the very nature of the sonnet's form encouraged its rapid cultural diffusion during the sixteenth and early seventeenth centuries. The sonnet, in effect, joined the standardized meters, such as the Italian hendecasyllable, the English pentameter, and the French alexandrine, that were beginning to assert their authority within the same period. All served as culturally accepted standards, laws of good poetry, but laws against which the poet was expected to articulate his or her own individualized voice. One may surmise that the sonnet achieved its particular status among poetic forms in two major ways. Most obviously, its recognized elements of rhyme and meter—canonized somewhat differently in each national literature—set into high relief minor differences, whether a modulation in theme, a change in rhetoric, or a novel tone. At the same time, the sonnet's form, replete with phonic and visual repetitions, lent a mastering closure to the poetic discourse and a coherence to the speaking voice, difficult to attain in more loosely structured lyric texts. Countless sonnet voices called for a hearing in the sixteenth and early seventeenth centuries. Together they moved in the direction of the solidifying ideals of middle-class culture: an easy freedom within constraint, a graceful containment of the individual within the larger community.

As the sonnet made its way from Italy to France and then later to England, it soon became less important that one imitated Petrarch exactly than that one respected the sonnet's norms: its formal particulars, its eloquent style, its sense of a strong poetic voice, and its idealizing courtly love themes. The *Rime sparse* was known, to be sure, but the models for apprentice writers came more often than not from minor Italian poets whose works had been compiled in collections known as the *Rime di diversi*.[15] In France, where the sonnet appeared first in the hands of Clément Marot (1496–1544) and Mellin de Saint-Gelais (1491–1558), the sonnet "myth" was visibly in action. The most illustrious poets of the day—Du Bellay, Ronsard, de Tyard, Baif, Jodelle, and Belleau—calling themselves the Pléiade, clustered at the Parisian courts of Francis I and, later, Henry II, and produced a self-consciously nationalistic poetics. With their backs to the medieval practice of earlier French vernacular literature, intricate rhyme schemes, earthy puns and all, they followed instead the Greeks, Romans, and Italians in an attempt to recreate classical perfection.[16] *Odi profanum vulgus* was their motto.

Du Bellay was the first to write sonnet sequences patterned to varying degrees on previous Italian examples—initially in the

Petrarchan *Olive*, and then in the far more original *Regrets* and *Antiquités de Rome*.[17] Still, only in Ronsard's sonnet cycles—the *Amours* of Cassandra, Marie, and Hélène—did the French Renaissance sonnet achieve its greatest influence.[18] Ronsard perfected the formal features of the French sonnet and established its classical form as one built entirely out of alexandrines. But at the same time that he strengthened the sonnet's "rules" in the interest of promoting an illustrious French poetry, his themes defied many of the tradition's accepted norms. Thus, though he performed gracefully as the more or less idealizing Petrarchan lover in the *Amours de Cassandre*, his sequence placed Grecian themes over the Latin ones favored by the Italians, as did to an even greater extent his much later *Sonnets pour Hélène*. But Ronsard could play the sensual lover as well, and the early *Amours de Marie* takes the Renaissance love themes in directions seldom traveled in the main Italian tradition. Led by poets such as these, and later by the mannerist Jean de Sponde, the French writers did achieve their goal: to change the concept of what good French poetry, even good French language, should be. They did so in considerable part through the sonnet.

The sonnet vogue arrived later in England, brought first from Italy by Wyatt (1503–42) and Surrey (1518–47). Praised by Puttenham for introducing the iambic pentameter and bringing English poetry somewhat nearer to classical perfection, Wyatt and Surrey seem on the surface to share the spiritual motivations of the French Renaissance poets who had taken up the sonnet some years before. As in France, in England sonnets were written in courtly circles. They were, in fact, part of a larger phenomenon, in which poetic effects emulated courtly behavior in elegance, eloquence, and beauty.[19] At times, they even served as a passport to an elite circle of courtiers and men of letters.[20] But England, already at a peak of commercial power and eager to prove its cultural attainments as well, prided itself on its literary past, and was less ready than France or Italy to reject a medieval literature in order to import new, more classical norms. Rather than turn against their medieval literary heritage, the English poets reworked it, bringing it to greater sophistication by weaving in a number of Italian and French strands. Thus, the English author might assume the traditional sonnet pose of a poet-lover singing or speaking to a lady. But his emphasis remained, from Wyatt's earliest translations on, generally more objective, realistic, earthly, and in keeping with the literature of the English medieval tradition.[21] Rejecting, for the most part, the idealizing strain common among writers of Italian and French sonnets, his language tended toward words more specific in meaning and more object-oriented in reference.

Although neither Wyatt nor Surrey composed a lyric sequence, the later English sonnet did eventually regain its accustomed role as a fragment within a larger whole. If anything, in their use of the sonnet sequence, English poets surpassed their counterparts in France and Italy—first through Sidney, in his *Astrophil and Stella*, then through the works of such poets as Daniel, Spenser, and Shakespeare himself.[22]

Shakespeare's sequence appeared at the very end of the English Renaissance sonnet vogue (1609 was the date of Thorpe's pirated edition, though most scholars agree that the poems were probably composed near the end of the sixteenth century),[23] and it derived much of its uniqueness from a particularly treasonous traditionalism. In form, his sonnets departed from the familiar octave-sestet patterns to revive Surrey's early variation (a sonnet of three separate quatrains and a closing couplet). The themes Shakespeare approaches—time, death and, above all, the complications and ambiguities of human relationships—developed some of the more realistic motifs already a part of the English tradition and indicative of a new literary practice coming into its own during the sixteenth and seventeenth centuries. In their mimetic qualities, Shakespeare's sonnets bring to a logical conclusion a major strain in English Renaissance writing. But certain Shakespearean effects strike a highly original note. For instance, although specific references to things and persons typify the Shakespearean text, these references frequently entail ambiguities and even contradictions of a sort seldom encountered in the works of either Petrarch or his followers. The disturbing, often paradoxical play of Shakespeare's wit and the open-ended nature of his sequence make the *Sonnets* undoubtedly the most complex and problematic lyric collection of the era. But nothing makes it more novel in the context of what came before than the poet's creation of a second person, a "thou," and with it, a series of dramatic encounters. Yet, ironically, as "Farewell! thou art too dear" itself suggests, this new emphasis often allows Shakespeare to weave into his treasonous sonnet writing a quality of love fully congenial to the conventional, idealizing patterns that came before.

THE DRAMA OF "I" AND "THOU"

Unlike Petrarch, Shakespeare was not averse to directly addressing his friend or mistress. In fact, the word "thou" occupies a prominent place in Shakespeare's lexicon, opening the sequence to an entirely new imaginative dimension. While the reader never forgets the distinctive voice of the sonnet text, he or she tends to hear it projecting outward, calling up the image of another.

Sonnet 87 shows Shakespeare's dramatic lyric in action. If the greater part of the sonnet stages an ironic rationalization of the speaker's farewell, the sonnet voice continually promotes a keen sense of human encounter. As he speaks, for instance, a grammatical alternation, in which "I" and "thou" take turns as subject, creates the effect of inner dialogue. Thus, the poet first plumbs the reasons for the fair youth's break, turns in quatrain two directly to himself, then turns again, putting "thou" in control of the third stanza for a pièce de résistance of mock explanation, only to close the sonnet with a couplet governed once more by "I."

However, this dialogical reasoning cannot alone account for the level of drama that Shakespeare achieves. The pervasive legal metaphor and the ambiguities it awakens also play a role. It is chiefly to them that the sonnet owes its ironic tone and its pronounced sense of the speaker's point of view. As a metaphoric code of legal terms justifies the young man's break, a case of personal affection and loss is virtually reduced to a legal contract and its cancellation. But a series of ambiguous couplings—entailing property and love, persons and things—marks an ironic difference between what is literally said and what the poet would have us believe. Beginning with "dear" and "possessing" in line 1, a quick succession of ambiguities (based on "estimate," "bonds," "charter," "releasing," and "determinate") reifies the young man and seals the sense of a very "deal" in affection. The reader, however, who retains the associations of line 1 (and perhaps demands whether a friend, even a highly placed one, can ever be "too dear") and who registers the pointedly ironic phrase "like as not" inserted in line 2, is not likely to take the speaker's words as an altogether serious rendition of human love. If anything, their irony seems to evince bitterness. Nor are the final quatrains calculated to lessen this effect.

If legal terms diminish in quatrain two (only "patent" and "granting" in line 5), the loved one's description as "that riches" and "this fair gift" nonetheless transforms him completely from a person into a "thing" of pecuniary worth. This reification works itself into a veritable reductio ad absurdum in the most grammatically involved third stanza. While practically restating the reasoning of previous lines, the stanza now attributes it directly to the fair young man whom the speaker, in a final ironic gesture, places in a commercial transaction in which the young man himself is the object of exchange. "Thy self thou gav'st" explicitly transforms the friend into a third person object of his own action, a reified self that reappears as "it" and "gift" in the following lines. If such reifications of love have not already created in the reader's mind a startling contrast with more conventionally idealized views of human affection, the couplet announces the disparity.

With the turn in rhyme scheme at line 13 comes the poem's only abrupt change in tone, and its single distinct foray beyond the legal reasoning of the quatrains. For suddenly the imagery of the couplet turns the developing irony against the speaking self. It conjures, first, a time before this "farewell!," recalling a past possession of the "other" and likening it to a dream in which the self was king. After such a vision, the final hemistich falls with the resounding thud of reality. Opposed to the dream and the past come the waking and, implicitly, the present. Instead of acting the king, the one human being powerful enough to be immune to a contractual bond, the self fades behind the anonymous negation, "no such matter." Irony turns inward to cast the dramatic bitterness of the quatrains into a starkly clarifying light. As the final iambs suggest, the argument of the quatrains has in fact done no more than dramatize a loss of the "other" that brings in its wake a loss of self.

Through the self-abnegating closure, the speaker thus ironically resurrects the sonnet tradition's more idealized views of love. Clearly at odds with the worldliness of the quatrains, he here reveals an intensely personal and deeply, even searingly felt, experience. In the process, Shakespeare's dramatic encounter, with all its distinctive metaphoric collisions of sense and their collusion with a public legal context, turns in the end to a yet more fundamental collusion with a conventionally idealizing view of love.

Of course, Shakespeare's metaphoric practice contributes to much more than the ironic effects we see in "Farewell! thou art too dear." In fact, its play of lively difference within repetitious overlaps of sense lends itself to enormous variations in imagery, tone, and meaning.

INVISIBLE DIFFERENCES

Probably no one has offered a better description of Shakespeare's rhetorical strategy than Coleridge: "Shakespeare's intellectual action is wholly unlike that of Ben Jonson or Beaumont and Fletcher. The latter see the totality of a sentence or passage, and then project it entire. Shakespeare goes on creating, and evolving B. out of A., and C. out of B., and so on, just as a serpent moves, which makes a fulcrum of its own body and seems forever twisting and untwisting its own strength."[24]

Corroborating this analysis, Stephen Booth describes reading a Shakespeare sonnet as a process of slipping from one frame of reference to another.[25] One might take yet another step in the same direction to say that if Shakespeare's technique is highly metaphorical (and this is, I believe, its most distinctive feature), it often shows metonymic qualities through a metamorphosis of imagery within the same sonnet and through a use of grammar to highlight and frame such transformations. Metaphors that are continually displaced and transformed into new metaphors create an "invisible syntax" within the reader's mind.

Were one to comb Shakespeare's *Sonnets* with an eye to rhetorical figures, one would in fact find much the same assortment of schemes and tropes as in Petrarch's *Rime sparse* or, for that matter, in the works of the contemporaries of Shakespeare whom Coleridge mentions. But the function and distribution of such figures differ markedly. Shakespeare's grammatical schemes, such as his numerous hyperbata and antitheses, manage not only to disclose varying psychological nuances of meaning, but, more importantly, to set up more spectacular tropes, to highlight the images they create, and to provide quick transitions from one sonnet "picture" to another. Put another way, Shakespeare's poetic effects display an inversion of the metaphor-metonymy relationship observed in Petrarch's sonnets. There, metaphor served metonymy. Here, metonymy serves a strong metaphoric emphasis.

Shakespeare's mental pictures themselves derive in part from the unusual range of vocabulary he invokes. They grow as well from his use of vivid tropes—synecdoche, metonymy and, most important, metaphor and pun. Synecdoches, fragmenting the speaking self or the addressee, and metonymies, displacing an emotion (such as love) with a bodily cause (the heart), shape many sonnets of praise and of love's effects on the poet. But though such figures may at times carry the weight of the sonnet's imagery, more often they serve as the tropological basis for metaphor itself, as in the third stanza of "Farewell! thou art too dear," where a synecdochic figure—"Thy self thou gav'st"—forms the basis of a more extensive metaphoric sequence.

Because of the often pyramidlike structure of Shakespeare's rhetoric, in which grammar and metonymic trope seem to exist only to help bring the master trope metaphor into prominence, it would be inappropriate to arrange grammatical schemes and tropes on a horizontal, metonymic plane as in Petrarch's case. To envision Shakespeare's rhetorical priorities, one would instead have to tip the line of figures into the vertical attitude used to suggest a dependence on the paradigmatic or metaphoric dimension of language and conceive of the Shakespearean rhetoric as a mass of figures—responsible for creating novel mental effects through constantly changing metaphoric pictures—moving forward in the time of the sonnet.

	linear movement of invisible syntax
paradigmatic (reader's imagination)	pun
	metaphor
	metonymy
	synecdoche
	oxymoron
	paradox
syntagmatic (vision of the text)	antithesis
	hyperbaton
	linear movement of visible syntagm

Pyramids of figures such as these, conveyed in a syntax itself complex and changeful, and used so that metaphoric tropes remain uppermost, generate an invisible syntax before the reader's inner eye. At the same time, they suggest the enormous importance that Shakespeare grants to the tropological or cognitive level of the text.

In his introductory sonnet, "From fairest creatures," for instance, Shakespeare relies heavily on metaphoric figures to create what Winifred Nowottney has termed a "litany of images."[26]

> From fairest creatures we desire increase,
> That thereby beauty's rose might never die,
> But as the riper should by time decease,
> His tender heir might bear his memory:
> But thou contracted to thine own bright eyes,
> Feed'st thy light's flame with self-substantial fuel,
> Making a famine where abundance lies,
> Thy self thy foe, to thy sweet self too cruel:
> Thou that art now the world's fresh ornament,
> And only herald to the gaudy spring,
> Within thine own bud buriest thy content,

And tender churl mak'st waste in niggarding:
Pity the world, or else this glutton be,
To eat the world's due, by the grave and thee.

The direct substitution of one lexical element for another produces images intended to jog the reader's mind into a series of analogies, all depicting the fair youth: "beauty's rose," "the riper," "glutton," for example. But metaphoric figures also emerge through contrasts between two or more words in a phrase (such as "Thy self thy foe," "Within thine own bud buriest thy content") that ask the reader to consider what underlying similarities link apparently disparate meanings. And, as we focus on the play of similarity and difference in our minds, words recede while imagined "things" appear, that re-present life's vividness and flux.

In this sonnet, no less than in sonnet 87, the more linear, metonymic thrust of language links words and projects figures to their best advantage. In the third quatrain, for instance, it spurs narcissism to rise up against nature in the course of a single line: "Within thine own bud buriest thy content." Here, the grammatical figure hyperbaton supports the imaginative scene, underscoring the metaphor by forming an alliterative kernel—"bud buriest"—at the very center of the line. In this way, both grammar and trope join to spark the imaginative life of the reader's mind.

Such a metonymic underpinning for a metaphoric text is but one example of the ways in which differential elements play a role in Shakespeare's poetics. From his distinctive use of the sonnet form, to his projection of varied, mobile, and often antithetical images in the course of individual sonnets and the collection as a whole, to the differences inscribed in a single word or image, Shakespeare presents a series of paradoxical counterpoints that creates in the invisible dimension of the reader's mind a lively sense of difference.

In the English sonnet's open three-part form, Shakespeare found a ready stage for the differential play he used to dramatize life's active flux. The English sonnet's structure—with its build of three quatrains capped by a couplet, all rhyming ABAB, CDCD, EFEF, GG—had, of course, been available since Surrey first used it in the 1530s and 1540s.[27] By the time Shakespeare chose the pattern, presumably in the 1590s, the genre had already been reworked and remodeled by the leading poets of the day. Reshaped by Sidney to a more constrained, more Italianate scheme (either ABAB, ABAB, CDCD, EE or ABAB, ABAB, CCD, EED) and revised again by Spenser into a barely more flexible shape (ABAB, BCBC, CDCD, EE), Surrey's older but much more open form apparently appealed most to Shakespeare, who found it suitable for all but three of his sonnets. Its greater number of end-rhymes and the formal detachment of each stanza encourage precisely the kind of dynamic changes in sound and idea in which Shakespeare specializes.

Equally important, the significance that the reader implicitly attaches to any poetic ending (one that Shakespeare's development of themes often accentuates) gains impact through the single change of pattern that the final rhyming couplet of Surrey's form brings. Since the major turn in the English sonnet comes only when the third quatrain gives way to the closing couplet, the form lacks the ample space for poetic conclusions that the Italian sestet affords. But it does seem bred precisely for the witty finale, the quick about-face in themes and sound of which Shakespeare was fond.

Apt for epigrammatic statement preceded by extended argument or for a series of images, the Shakespearean sonnet form allows more room for poetic experiment than the other current English patterns, and more by far than the more rigidly rhymed Petrarchan sonnet. But it also requires a particularly deft hand to exploit its capacity for extended thematic development and curb its penchant toward monotony.

In fact, Shakespeare easily avoids monotony by using the English sonnet's repetitious verse form to stage grammatical and semantic differences. In "From fairest creatures," for instance, opposing forces of natural life and narcissistic death align themselves in the opening stanzas and then play out their differences in semantic action that culminates at the poem's conclusion. Thus, the initial quatrain with its figures of healthy natural reproduction—"beauty's rose," "the riper," "tender heir,"—must face, in quatrain two, a threatening mass of more complex images accusing the youth of self-destructive narcissism: "thou contracted to thine own bright eyes," "Feed'st thy light's flame with self-substantial fuel," "Thy self thy foe," "to thy sweet self too cruel." Quatrain three drives on with nature imagery recalling the first stanza—"world's fresh ornament," "herald to the gaudy spring"—and juxtaposes an imagery that strongly evokes the narcissistic: "Within thine own bud buriest thy content" and "tender churl mak'st waste in niggarding."

But it is not simply that the quickly moving contrasts, and thus the differential structure, of Shakespeare's introductory sonnet characterize many other single poems; the particular antitheses he presents themselves extend to the sequence as a whole. The poet inveighs against narcissism, and urges reincarnation in another in almost every one of the first seventeen sonnets. At times, these themes act as direct warnings to the youth. Shakespeare writes in sonnet 6, "Be not self-willed for thou art much too fair, / To be death's conquest and make worms thine heir." At other moments, such as in sonnets 3 and 11, the effects of the youth's self-content take on more massive social and historical proportions. Sonnet 3 asks, "Or who is he so fond will be the tomb, / Of his self-love to stop posterity?" Sonnet 11 makes a similar point: "If all were minded so, the times should cease, / And threescore years would make the world away." But the theme of narcissism as an unnatural, as well as self-defeating act figures most prominently in sonnet 4. Here, the paradoxical image, "mak'st waste in niggarding," first presented in sonnet 1, builds into a metaphorical chain no less consistent, and no less threatening to the notion of "true love," than the legal imagery of "Farewell! thou art too dear":

> Unthrifty loveliness why dost thou spend,
> Upon thy self thy beauty's legacy?
> Nature's bequest gives nothing but doth lend,
> And being frank she lends to those are free:
> Then beauteous niggard why dost thou abuse,
> The bounteous largess given thee to give?

The Shakespearean Sonnet / 69

> Profitless usurer why dost thou use
> So great a sum of sums yet canst not live?
> For having traffic with thy self alone,
> Thou of thy self thy sweet self dost deceive,
> Then how when nature calls thee to be gone,
> What acceptable audit canst thou leave?
>> Thy unused beauty must be tombed with thee,
>> Which uséd lives th'executor to be.

Of one thing the speaker is certain, here and in other sonnets as well—such love of self is not love at all. He elaborates in sonnet 9, "No love toward others in that bosom sits / That on himself such murd'rous shame commits," and follows in sonnet 10, "Grant if thou wilt, thou art beloved of many, / But that thou none lov'st is most evident." What does constitute love in the Shakespeare sequence? Certainly not self-hoarding, nor even the poetically fruitful self-contemplation characteristic of Petrarch's poetry. It is instead a love that reaches out to another, that itself admits difference.

In the course of the sonnets, such a love is cast first and foremost in terms of natural reproduction. The "husbandry" urged in the first group of sonnets is intended to produce an earthly self-reincarnation, a second self that blunts the threat of time and establishes whatever claim human beings can have to immortality. It is this refrain that, sounding in the course of the sonnets as a whole, stands out with particular clarity in the final lines of sonnet 16:

> So should the lines of life that life repair
> Which this (Time's pencil) or my pupil pen
> Neither in inward worth nor outward fair
> Can make you live your self in eyes of men.
>> To give away your self, keeps your self still,
>> And you must live drawn by your own sweet skill.

This losing oneself in love of another only to find a greater immortality in a child trims the familiar Christian paradox, with its reference to life-giving death, to thoroughly earthly proportions.

Such a paradoxical, differential description of love is anything but a passing fancy in the Shakespeare collection. If the theme of reproduction ends with the seventeenth sonnet, the theme of an earthly reincarnation through selfless love goes on. And, with it, the countervailing threat posed by a selfish love. A self-giving love, precarious though it is, dominates the first 126 sonnets addressed to the young man. A love that itself can conquer time, it carries with it the familiar images of natural cycles, husbandry, truth, and beauty that Shakespeare developed in sonnets 1 to 17.[28] Similarly, in the sonnets to the dark woman, which explore themes of a purely sexual love and selfish motives, the negative imagery of worldliness, death, hoarding, falsehood, and ugliness reappear in full force.[29]

But beyond these already pervasive thematic lines, Shakespeare's presentation of love as reincarnation amounts to perhaps the most effective metaphor for Shakespeare's poetics as a whole.[30] As more than a few sonnets declare, Shakespeare's poetry itself claims to be an immortalization of sorts, a renewal and re-presentation of life through words. And in its purely verbal reincarnation, it takes on the qualities the poet attributes to love. Sonnets as different as "Shall I compare thee to a summer's day?," "Like as the waves make towards the pebbled shore," and "Since brass, nor stone, nor earth, nor boundless sea," all celebrate the poet's art as a principal means to the young man's immortality. It is true that poetry remains for Shakespeare little more than a secondary sort of eternity, too much the "tomb" and "monument" to offer the comfort one might wish. It is also true that Shakespeare grants this immortalizing privilege only to a very particular type of poem, one that mirrors and preserves as much of life's truth as possible. As he writes in sonnet 101, "Then do thy office Muse, I teach thee how, / To make him seem long hence, as he shows now."

But whether or not Shakespeare honestly believed that his art could do little more than serve as a "lettered monument," he was certainly well aware that the repetition of written words over time grants them what might be described as a perpetual renewal of life. Not only does Shakespeare present the theme of poetic reproduction in a number of sonnets, he seems to employ every linguistic means at his disposal to project life's various, often contradictory, dimensions and to involve his reader in experiencing them. Not unlike the self-giving differential love that serves as the central thematic ideal of Shakespeare's sequence, poetry is itself meant to effect a complex reincarnation, a regeneration of life's differential flux. In its efforts to achieve this, not only its metaphoric vividness but its metonymic fluctuations play a role. By recourse to a linear run or transformation of metaphors, by an inclination to image-making whereby "A gives way to B and B to C," Shakespeare succeeds in making his verbal pictures disturbingly evanescent. One metaphor barely appears before another overtakes it. A principal effect of this rapid substitution—one that occurs in "From fairest creatures," but even more intensely in later sonnets such as "That time of year"—is that a full presence of meaning nearly always stands just beyond reach.

Such constant creation and destruction of meaning may give Shakespeare's sonnets a particularly modern texture. But in the context of the collection, its themes and images, these rapid transformations contribute to a quite traditional mimetic purpose. Shakespeare's invisible syntax, carrying in its wake his differential themes, may just as well be read as a poetic presentation of the ongoing movement of time itself. The end of each sonnet brings with it the end of a fragment of artistic life.

For this reason Shakespeare doubtless prized the sonnet form as much for its brevity as for its flexible shape. Like time in the natural world, his sonnets give the images of life only a brief course to run before they end, to be succeeded by others, no less riddled by difference and contradiction than those that came before. And almost all are presented through a lyric voice that itself manages to be differential, asking the reader to fictionalize not only a rapidly changing series of images and the poetic voice serving as their imagined source, but also the "other" to whom the poet addresses himself. We imagine a dialogue, sometimes even envision a drama.

From the imaginative presence of lover and beloved, perhaps the most salient feature of the *Sonnets*, comes a major difference between Shakespeare's poetics and that of the *Rime sparse*. Shakespeare's use of the grammatical second person and modes of discourse that imply a listener—such as apostrophes, imperatives, and interrogatives—adds unusual dramatic density to what we have called in our reading of Petrarch the performative level of the text. Far from an autoreflexive monologue, managed by an omnipotent "I," the Shakespearean sonnet constitutes a veritable stage for interpersonal communication. The power of Shakespeare's metaphoric or cognitive figures only heightens our ability to imagine two persons. Seldom dominated by a single, powerful and thematically pervasive first person voice, Shakespeare's sonnet opens itself to the imaginative difference of a second person.

Actually, Shakespeare's portrait of an "I" and a "thou" distinguishes his sonnets almost as radically from his English predecessors as from Petrarch himself. Spenser and Daniel, following Petrarch, had given the first person voice almost unique control of the lyric collection. Even Sidney and Drayton who, like Shakespeare, recognize both an "I" and a "thou," in fact rarely charge their sonnets with the sort of human drama Shakespeare prizes. Although "thou" does figure in their lyrics, the word rarely evokes images of the loved one, but rather of friends or even personified qualities. When Shakespeare charges his sonnets with the second grammatical person—as is the case in 118 of his 154 sonnets—he does so almost invariably to address the fair young man or dark lady.[31]

Why the new, dramatic direction that Shakespeare brings to the sonnet tradition? Not the least important factor is the new era in which he writes. His forceful emphasis upon a "thou" is one important sign of an artistic era no longer so fettered by religious constraints. Petrarch and those who followed in Italy, France, and England, had long since forged a place for the secular poet and his frankly secular loves. By the 1590s, when Shakespeare was writing, the poet could quite comfortably extend his reach to another member of a now more classically human, more earthly community, without fear of jeopardizing his authorial status.

But time alone could never account fully for the high drama of Shakespeare's poetics. Other factors must also be weighed. To the humanistic reach generally available to the sixteenth-century poet, Shakespeare added a personal break with the English tradition of the poet-courtier. The first English sonnets had in fact been written by the noblemen Wyatt, Surrey, and Sidney. Only later had middle-class poets taken up the form, competing—largely by imitation—with the earlier nobles and frequently using the sonnet as a possible means to courtly preferment.[32] Writing not only for the glory of a noble patron, but ultimately for their own, middle-class poets such as Drayton and Spenser tended to a "high" poetic style marked by eloquent rhetoric and expressions of respect. A most effective means, of course, of achieving a distant and respectful tone was the avoidance of direct address altogether in favor of impersonal, third person forms. Shakespeare, whose sonnets were not the sort to gain him the favor of the nobleman he addressed, never in fact even sought the poetic recognition that might come from a proper publication of his sequence. But beyond that, setting himself sharply apart from the rhetorical practice of the poet-courtier, he addressed his objects of love as "thou," directly and frankly, as one human being to another, and without the respectful detachment that had become traditional.

Still more important, Shakespeare's dramatic lyric style served his larger poetic aims. It is, for one, precisely the sort of lyric style one would expect from a poet whose primary literary activity has been playwriting. In Shakespeare's *Sonnets*, as in his plays, the performative level of the text, with its build of a "thou" as well as an "I," does not undermine his differential imagery or its cognitive import. The ultimate effect of "thou" is, in fact, to add yet another invisible dimension to the poetic discourse, and to use this dimension to frame complex plays of sonnet imagery in all-pervasive, recognizable patterns of human relationship and dramatic encounter. In this sense, Shakespeare's dialogical sonnet style rings entirely consistent with his rhetoric as a whole.

In this most fundamental and most recurrent linguistic structure, Shakespeare's kaleidoscopic imagery finds a referential home. Seldom do third person nouns or metaphors serve, as they do in the *Rime sparse*, as metonymic surrogates for an absent, displaced beloved. Still less often do they stand alone, conjuring their own, impersonal world. Shakespeare's imagery rarely builds an impersonal world since his metaphors almost always contribute to our imaging one or more of the three central sonnet personae. In sonnets such as "Your love and pity," for instance, thematic material becomes part and parcel of the dramatic "characters" and their situations:

> Your love and pity doth th'impression fill,
> Which vulgar scandal stamped upon my brow,
> For what care I who calls me well or ill,
> So you o'er-green my bad, my good allow?
> You are my all the world, and I must strive,
> To know my shames and praises from your tongue;
> None else to me, nor I to none alive,
> That my steeled sense or changes right or wrong.
> In so profound abysm I throw all care
> Of others' voices, that my adder's sense,
> To critic and to flatterer stoppéd are:
> Mark how with my neglect I do dispense.
>   You are so strongly in my purpose bred,
>   That all the world besides methinks are dead.

If a good number of the sonnet's third person references point synecdochically to abstract emotions or qualities—"love," "pity," "bad," "good," "shames," "praises," "sense," "purpose," "neglect"—all are grammatically tied to the "I" or "thou" through possessive pronouns. And if other sonnet nouns instead help sketch the dramatic situation, drawing in the backdrop for the developing interaction—words such as "impression," "scandal," "world," "abysm," "care," "voices," "critics," "flatterer"—these too bend grammatically either to the lyric "I" or the addressee. "Impression" and "scandal" build images in a grammar dominated by subjects "possessed" by the second person; "world" in the second quatrain is incorporated in a phrase belonging to "I," while even "abysm," "voices," "critics," "flatterer," and "world" (that is, when "world" recurs in the couplet) participate in phrases grammatically governed by the first person.[33] The very fact that a "thou" may, and frequently does, grammatically dominate Shakespeare's imagery, accounts at least in part for one of the poet's most important semantic effects. For it is through this rhetorical device that the object of love in the Shakespearean poem acquires its exceptional autonomy and thematic power. The dominance of "thou" is essential to creating the image of the speaker's all-encompassing and selfless love. And the consequent receding of "I" only encourages Shakespeare's abundant imagery to cling more closely to the beloved "other."

All this is not to say that the speaking voice ever effaces itself entirely. Just as in thematic terms, Shakespeare's image of a selfless love serves above all to extend the self, allowing it, so to speak, to live twice and to live more fully, the presence of a powerful "thou" in his grammar inevitably implies the speaker, the one who calls the other into being through the very act of speech. For all the imaginative space given to the fair youth and the dark mistress, these figures remain ultimately part of the speaker's world. In this sense, Shakespeare's "two loves" provide an imaginative vehicle for the persona, the "I." Evoked by Shakespeare's dialogical grammar and supported by a realistic imagery, they amount to an extended metaphor within the *Sonnets*, a means of conjuring in the reader's mind a relationship of the speaker to other human beings and, through this extension, of reincarnating the speaking voice itself.

In this sense, we see another fascinating counterpoint with Petrarch's rhetoric. There, a single voice controlled the imagery. A voice we might have expected to be a simple metaphor, it proved to be changing, questing, always incomplete—as metonymic as the statements it traced and the themes it evoked. In Shakespeare's text, difference is fashioned otherwise, more metaphorically, through the dramatic encounters of three separately imagined persons: the speaker, the young man, and the young woman. Though the voice here does not trace a trajectory of desire in search of self, it does seek definition through its own sort of difference—its relationship to other human beings who, presented in the sonnets as separate beings, nonetheless help concretize qualities, attitudes, aspirations even, of the speaking self.

The sonnet "Your love and pity" perfectly expresses the inseparability of "I" and "thou." In the course of fourteen lines, the fair youth's role changes from that of an independent figure to the animating soul of the speaking self. If the youth's act of forgiveness dominates the opening quatrain, the second stanza brings the words, "You are my all the world," in which the poet explicitly defines himself through this image of an other. At least from the lover's perspective, the youth encompasses all reality. He blunts the impact of worldly criticism and simultaneously offers the poet a medium of self-knowledge. For the rest of the sonnet, the poet explores the effect of this newfound self-measure, making the youth literally a part of the speaking self. By the time "you" appears in the closing couplet, he lives only in his lover's psyche; he is "in [his] purpose bred." From this internalized "god of love," as the poet calls the youth in sonnet 110, he will take his moral cues and derive his sense of self.

Shakespeare's dramatic lyricism, here and in the vast majority of his sonnets, makes it possible for him to draw a powerfully anthropocentric universe in which human beings define themselves purely in terms of human relationships. The drama only grows through the creation of several poetic clusters within the *Sonnets* as a whole. Some of the most successful discussions of the sonnet sequence go in fact beyond its broad themes, such as love and time, to attend to the various dramatic scenes that lend it its vividness.[34] The action of a slender and stable cast of three main dramatis personae—the poet-speaker, the fair nobleman, the dark mistress—produces no fewer than seven distinct thematic groups: (1) the marriage group, (2) the poet's absence, (3) the friend's fault, (4) the poet's fault, (5) the rival poet, (6) the immortalization, and (7) the mistress sonnets.

Just as "Farewell! thou art too dear" speaks to the question of the rival poet, and as "From fairest creatures" belongs to the marriage group, "Your love and pity" is the culmination of a four-sonnet dramatic scene focusing on the poet's fault. Thus, the first line of the poem, "Your love and pity doth th'impression fill," conveys the fair youth's responsiveness to the poet's admission of fault and his plea for love and pity, both already expressed in sonnets 109 and 110. And though the poet's wrong is never clearly identified, it seems to bear some relationship to the playwright's and actor's craft whose demeaning qualities are the subject of sonnets 110 and 111.

Such dramatic scenes, each presenting at least two characters, reinforce the human import of Shakespeare's grammar and imagery. True, the speaker's love for the youth develops at times into a distinctly platonizing love, and his feelings for the mistress into a mockery of sexual desire. True again, the sequence is thoroughly charged with powerful oppositional dyads—life and death, spirit and flesh, "heaven and hell," "comfort and despair." Still, Shakespeare's focus on specific situations and interpersonal events keeps such oppositions from rigidifying into fixed, abstract schemes. Thanks to his balance of a realistic lexicon and what might be termed a humanistic grammar, the major themes remain sensually present, ostensibly real. Shakespeare's grammatically bound imagery joins sonnets into thematic groups and, at times, to more extrinsic sociohistorical questions.

References to the actor's craft appearing in sonnets 109 to 112, for instance, prompt the reader to consider the role of the playwright and actor in Shakespeare's day. The word "motley" in sonnet 110, and the reference in sonnet 111 to "public means which public manners breeds" and to "nature . . . subdued / To what it works in, like the dyer's hand," all have traditionally been interpreted biographically and historically on the knowledge that Shakespeare himself was an actor and a playwright and that both were considered vulgar professions in his day. As Stephen Booth puts it:

> Shakespeare's profession is—and presumably always was—known to his readers . . . and this line [line 2 of sonnet 110] therefore is colored by (and colors the following lines with) its pertinence to the particular circumstances of its author's life. The fact of Shakespeare's profession operates—much as

the accident of his first name does in the "Will" sonnets (57, 89, 135, 136, 143)—to give witty, pun-like extra dimension to statements complete and meaningful in themselves.[35]

Most often, Shakespeare's semantic particularity and openness in the working out of dramatic situations point only more specifically to what I described as Shakespeare's mimetic use of metaphor and the referential overlaps it implies. But at times, and particularly in some of Shakespeare's most witty sonnets, referentiality is made problematic rather than reinforced. Rhetorical devices like pun and paradox seem to pry language loose from its referential frame and question the very possibility of mimesis.

Sonnets such as "That thou hast her it is not all my grief," "Whoever hath her wish, thou hast thy will," and "Take all my loves, my love, yea take them all" doubtless triggered the disparaging views of those eighteenth-century critics who regarded Shakespeare's rampant conceits and insistent wordplay with ill-concealed distaste. For Dr. Johnson, "a quibble was to [Shakespeare] the fatal Cleopatra for which he lost the world and was content to lose it."[36] And Stevens found in these sonnets "such labored perplexities and such studied deformities of style" that he chose not to reprint them in 1793, in the thought that "the strongest act of parliament that could be framed would fail to compel readers into their service."[37] Questioning every effort to arrive at a "proper" meaning, one translatable in terms of our everyday expectations, Shakespeare's wittiest metaphors seem to shun mimetic reference in favor of a purer verbal world of their own. Consider, for example, his sonnet, "Take all my loves":

> Take all my loves, my love, yea take them all,
> What hast thou then more than thou hadst before?
> No love, my love, that thou mayst true love call,
> All mine was thine, before thou hadst this more:
> Then if for my love, thou my love receivest,
> I cannot blame thee, for my love thou usest,
> But yet be blamed, if thou this self deceivest
> By wilful taste of what thy self refusest.
> I do forgive thy robbery gentle thief

> Although thou steal thee all my poverty:
> And yet love knows it is a greater grief
> To bear love's wrong, than hate's known injury.
>   Lascivious grace, in whom all ill well shows,
>   Kill me with spites yet we must not be foes.

The ambiguities that literally rage in the course of the sonnet, drawing from critics' widely disparate opinions of its worth,[38] depend primarily upon a massing of puns and paradoxes. Anything but extrinsic to Shakespeare's rhetoric as we have seen it so far, such figures in fact epitomize his metaphoric practice. They bring into particularly sharp focus his play on similarity-in-difference and difference-in-similarity. In the pun, a single sign acts as the perceptible pivot of a broad and varied associative space, the visible locus of invisible overlaps of sense. Here, "love" actually points to at least three interrelated and possible referents: the speaker's emotion, the addressee (the fair young man), and the absent mistress. The reader must choose one or more according to the context in which the word appears.

If Shakespeare's pun figures the play of difference-in-similarity in its most condensed form, his paradox captures the mirror image. Whereas a pun arises through the overlapping associations harbored in a single lexical element, a paradox (and its yet more compressed form, the oxymoron) is born out of two distinctly different, even opposite, lexical elements that can, however, be reconciled through a limited semantic overlap of sense in the invisible, associative region of the reader's mind. In this way, a "seemingly self-contradictory statement . . . is shown to be (sometimes in a surprising way) true."[39] Thus, when the paradox, "all mine was thine" demands that "mine" and "thine" point to opposite, self-contradictory referents, the sonnet nonetheless allows them to intersect, precisely in a "love" that joins them.

Since both pun and paradox rely heavily on the reader's associations, their pairing in a single text enormously heightens its intensity. In "Take all my loves," which describes the young man's fault as a theft of the poet's mistress, such intensity is hardly misplaced. "Take all my loves," in fact, makes the very ambiguity played out in puns on "love" the basis for a paradoxical, surprisingly true argument. If "love" recurs ten times in the course of the text, and always as a substantive, the repetitions are, nonetheless, fraught with difference. The sonnet's meaning depends in large part on subtle variations, and combinations, of its referents. Often, more than one of the three referents function simultaneously. At times, two become absolutely essential even to grasp the barest meaning of a phrase.

Shakespeare's puns on "love" come to a climax in lines 5 and 6, where the word occurs three times. The difficulty of these lines grows in part from syntactic displacement, in part from the ambiguity of two other words, but above all from the fact that "love" must incorporate more than one sense at a time in order for the phrase to have its meaning. Even assuming that "for" in line 5 means "on the grounds that" while "for" in line 6 means "because" or "since," and recalling that "usest" has strong sexual connotations,[40] the overall sense of the phrase remains polyvalent because of the multiple referents of "love": "Then if you have received 'my love' on the grounds that she/it is 'my love' (and all 'my loves' are thine), I cannot blame thee because you are using that which belongs to you (i.e., my love)." Although we can be quite sure that the first instance of "my love" in this reconstruction refers to the mistress, in the other two instances, the double meaning of the poet's emotion and the fair young man must be retained for the phrase to make sense. In short, the argument is both true and witty because the word "love" carries more than one meaning.

If the pun dominates the reasoning of quatrain two, the paradox and its compressed relation, the oxymoron, organizes stanzas one, three, and four. Like the pun, these figures focus on the meaning of "love." The sonnet's first quatrain strikes the central theme of a theft of love—but in a quick succession of apparent contradictions. The initial two lines frame a paradoxical query ("Take all my loves . . . What hast thou then more than thou hadst before?"), answered only by another paradoxical statement ("All mine was thine, before thou hadst this more"). Serving as the logical basis for subsequent reasoning, this statement finds its truth in the only human experience where all "mine" is "thine," the emotion so often evoked in the course of the sonnet and called by the name "love."

The paradoxical pattern of quatrain three lends weight to the speaker's accusations. No longer dubbed "my love," the youth now appears, oxymoronically, as a "gentle thief," and "taking" metamorphoses into a "robbery" that paradoxically "steal[s] thee all my poverty." But in spite of the blame that the poet's diction conveys, the reader does not forget that this amorous thief is still termed "gentle" (not only because he is noble, but quite simply because he is loved) and that what he steals is called "poverty" (since all of worth has already been given him, as "love").

Of all the sonnet paradoxes, Shakespeare saves his most telling for last. In a phrase that explains the paradoxical wit of the preceding quatrains, the poet states quite simply that, regardless of wrong, lover and loved one "must not be foes." A love in which "all mine is thine" is, by definition, not susceptible to theft.

Witty wordplay such as this, which earned Shakespeare a degree of infamy in the eighteenth century, might be defined far more charitably today, as an example of his extraordinary lexical sense, of what Ezra Pound called *logopoeia*: "'The dance of the intellect among words,' that is to say, it employs words not only for their direct meaning, but it takes count in a special way of habits of usage, of the context we expect to find with the word, its usual concomitants, of its known acceptances, and of ironical play. It holds the aesthetic content which is peculiarly the domain of verbal manifestation, and cannot possibly be contained in plastic or in music."[41]

In Shakespeare's logopoetic discourse, the music that arises from well-managed syntax and the visual design generated by metaphor merge into a complex play upon meaning and reference. And as in any text that highlights the problematic references of words, Shakespeare questions, to some extent at least, our notion of the "presence" to which his words refer. But in his provocative logopoeia, fraught as it is with innumerable semantic differences that challenge our notions of clear, unequivocal meaning, the problem of reference nonetheless remains surprisingly contained. In the *Sonnets*, semantic play is eventually bound, and its vagaries curbed, by the recurrent lyric drama itself, with its three personae and the definitions of "love" that join them. This emerges clearly enough in "Take all my loves." Paradox and pun work so effectively here because just as the paradoxes resolve in the ultimate generosity that Shakespeare gives to the word "love," so the word "love" is, quite literally, the linguistic "place" where the three sonnet personae meet. If there is ambiguity, it extends only so far as the dramatic situation itself—a situation that Shakespeare has bounded by words and their overlaps of sense.

Through such dramatic containment of a wide-ranging and changeful metaphoric dimension, Shakespeare's sonnets achieve their distinctive quality both as exemplars of an unusually generous-minded anthropocentric practice and as unusually vivid and complex expressions of love. Because of the framing bonds of "love," the multiple collisions of imagery at work in the Shakespearean sonnet are grounded in a collusion with a fully understandable human experience.

THE FINAL TURN OF THE RENAISSANCE SONNET MYTH

Though Shakespeare's art differs from Petrarch's in almost every respect, it would be hard to deny that it uses the sonnet form as effectively. Consistent with a metaphoric rhetoric in which difference constantly enlivens repetition, Shakespeare takes the principle of repetition and difference to the very heart of the sonnet's form. By so doing, he adds variety to the long and potentially monotonous expanse of three quatrains and sets into high relief the drama of the sonnet turn.

If stanza one poses the sonnet theme, stanza two is likely to bring a digression, complication, or striking contrast. The third quatrain generally perpetuates this additional complexity as it echoes themes already established in the initial four lines. Though Shakespeare's couplets often introduce still another analogy or opposition, his closures, as critics have been quick to note, perhaps strike one most through their grammatical and semantic simplicity.[42]

More important, though, than any semantic or grammatical contrasts to which one can point in Shakespeare's *Sonnets*, is his distinctive use of the performative dimension of the text. Not only does it lend a dramatic quality to the sonnets as a whole; it also emphasizes, if in a somewhat different way than the usual Petrarchan sonnet form, the moment of the sonnet turn. As the Shakespearean form itself would suggest, neither "I" nor "thou" regularly punctuates the sonnet center. But whatever the first twelve lines of the English sonnet may bring by way of enunciative pattern, Shakespeare's final couplet conjures an imaginative immediacy that can only come from a personalizing voice. At the close of a dramatic encounter that has drawn the reader through an often demanding poetic experience, the poet steps forward to speak—either directly to the loved one or simply to himself. In the process, the differential imagery that has characterized the sonnet up to that point resolves in a human and, generally, quite conventional context. In only 15 of the 154 sonnets does Shakespeare forego this dramatic potential to conclude the sonnet with a third person statement.[43]

For all their marked differences, then, in rhetorical and semantic transformation, the Petrarchan and Shakespearean structures bear an important resemblance. In both, the sonnet turn brings with it a distinct personal voice. Though the brevity of Shakespeare's second sonnet part does not allow for a developed change of thought such as we see in the sestet of Petrarch's form, in almost every case, these concluding lines reveal more clearly than anywhere else in the text the meaning that the preceding sonnet drama holds for the lyric self or his view of love. Whatever challenge Shakespeare's metaphoric quatrains may have posed to notions of meaning or the love convention itself, the final couplet is there to provide, if nothing more, the reassuring and referentially grounding image of a personal rapport.

Each of the sonnets examined in detail in the preceding pages concludes this way. If a direct first person form gives sonnet 87 its final ironic twist, the imperative (with its address to "thou") governs the close of sonnet 1, urging the young man to procreate. The couplet of sonnet 40 follows the grammatical pattern of sonnet 1. But here the imperative emphasizes the speaker's abiding love for the one who has wronged him, driving home the selflessness attached to the word "love." After a three stanza drama of "I" and "thou," the closing lines of sonnet 112 testify to the young man's presence in the poet's psyche by giving equal grammatical weight to both personae.

Just as Shakespeare modified the Petrarchan sonnet form but did not alter its length or the distinctive drama of its turn, he also modified the inherited Petrarchan themes, but did not destroy the already strong sense of tradition. Addressing both a fair young man and a dark mistress, Shakespeare did not really deny the by then outworn theme of an idealized Petrarchan love so much as draw out some of its more extreme and problematic features. The young man offers a perfect means to portray a compelling but even more sexually remote, even more spiritualized love than the preceding sonnet tradition ever expressed for the idealized female.[44] On the other hand, the dark mistress ("dark," the poet writes, in deeds as well as hue) allows Shakespeare to address directly the sexual ambiguity of courtly love. The frank sexuality almost always left obscure in the Petrarchan tradition as an unattainable, if not immoral, possibility, here receives explicit treatment, at times marked with humor and understanding, at times with revulsion and anxiety. By distinguishing two sides of human love in two contrasting figures, Shakespeare effectively expands and humanizes the powerful psychological drama concealed within the Petrarchan tradition. And in the process of rewriting centuries old themes in a new, more searching form, he effectively signals the final turn, the capping closure, of the sonnet tradition's Renaissance phase.

No one seems to have been more aware than Shakespeare himself that the *Sonnets* were a late contribution to the sonnet vogue. Early plays such as *Romeo and Juliet, The Two Gentlemen of*

Verona, and *Love's Labour's Lost* already found him mocking the by then aged Petrarchan sonnet vogue with its themes of a languishing lover and inaccessible mistress. And although Shakespeare evidently thought enough of the sonnet's potential to devote his energies to exploring it, a good many of his sonnets consciously confront the tradition through rhetorical maneuvers whose impact depends precisely upon the reader's knowledge of the sonnet's conventions. Not that Shakespeare offers any startlingly new criticisms of the tradition. A strong anti-Petrarchism had long flourished. From Berni in Italy to Du Bellay in France, to John Donne and Sir John Davies in England, it enlisted a healthy number of well-known writers. But more ably than others, Shakespeare managed to work a direct critique of sonnet clichés into a serious sonnet sequence and to use these parodic interludes to underscore his own originality.

Shakespeare marks his difference from lesser authors through several parodic asides in the first 126 sonnets.[45] But the final twenty-eight sonnets addressed to the mistress include his most direct and most humorous barbs. "My mistress' eyes," for instance, mocks the outworn tradition as it pays the nontraditional dark lady an honest, if hardly Petrarchan, compliment:

> My mistress' eyes are nothing like the sun,
> Coral is far more red, than her lips red,
> If snow be white, why then her breasts are dun;
> If hairs be wires, black wires grow on her head:
> I have seen roses damasked, red and white,
> But no such roses see I in her cheeks,
> And in some perfume is there more delight,
> Than in the breath that from my mistress reeks.
> I love to hear her speak, yet well I know,
> That music hath a far more pleasing sound.
> I grant I never saw a goddess go,
> My mistress when she walks treads on the ground.
>   And yet, by heaven, I think my love as rare,
>   As any she belied with false compare.

Sonnet structure, rhetoric, and even lexicon conspire here to parody certain dated Petrarchan effects and, in the process, to strike a new, more humanistic note. In contrast to the usual lively pattern of oppositions, for instance, this Shakespearean sonnet works by a simple structural repetition. As each line proceeds, sounding this sonnet mistress' distance from the courtly ideal, the train of quatrains offers no refreshing digressions, but at most a slight modulation of what has come before. In their clear break with Shakespeare's usual procedure, such semantic repetitions provide a structural souvenir of the sonnet's potential for imprisoning the discourse, a potential which Petrarch worked to obvious advantage in "Pace non trovo," but which later writers all too frequently abused. As if to mark more pointedly some of the most glaring abuses of the late sonnet tradition, Shakespeare enlists well-worn Petrarchan figures and vocabulary.

In flagrant opposition to his usual dramatic syntax of imagery, Shakespeare here mimics the Petrarchan device of the distanced, synecdochic anatomy of the lady. He even employs a recognizably Petrarchan lexicon for his parodic praise of each female feature. Eight idealizing metaphors and comparisons—all comparing the lady's "parts" with natural and supernatural beauties—are patiently negated by as many variations on "not." If most of these images had in fact entered the sonnet tradition with the popularization of the *Rime sparse*, almost all still held prominent places 250 years later in the Petrarchan sonnets of Shakespeare's lesser contemporaries. Consider, for instance, Henry Constable's hyperbolic enumeration of his lady's charms:

> One Sunne unto my lives day gives true light,
> One Moone dissolves my stormie night of woes.
> One starre my fate and happy fortune shoes.
> One Saint I serve, one shrine with vowes I dight.
> One sunne transfixt, hath burnt my hart outright.
> One Moone opposed, my love in darkness throes.
> One star hath bid my thoughtes my wrongs disclose.
> Saints scorn poor swaines, shrines doe my vowes no right.[46]

Or a sonnet such as this by Bartholomew Griffin, whose own sense of humor must have begged Shakespeare to cap it:

> My lady's hair is threads of beaten gold,
> Her front the purest crystal eye hath seen,
> Her eyes the brightest stars the heavens hold,
> Her cheeks red roses such as seld have been;
> Her pretty lips of red vermilion dye,
> Her hand of ivory the purest white,
> Her blush Aurora or the morning sky,
> Her breast displays two silver fountains bright,
> The spheres her voice, her grace the graces three;
> Her body is the saint that I adore;
> Her smiles and favors sweet as honey be;
> Her feet fair Thetis praiseth evermore.
> But oh, the worst and last is yet behind
> For of a griffin does she bear the mind.[47]

"My mistress' eyes" indeed starts off merely by negating the well-worn metaphors. But it gradually takes on a more original, more typically Shakespearean shape. The synecdoches that anatomize the mistress in quatrain one change by quatrain three into more comprehensive descriptions of her person. At the same time, outright negations yield to more neutral observations as the poetic voice slowly builds a personal point of view into a conventionally impersonal sonnet of praise. As we might expect, the closing couplet expresses most clearly Shakespeare's own perspective on his mistress and, at the same time, on the trite sonnet hyperboles he has systematically denied. The poet's device here is simple and perfectly appropriate to the pattern he has established in the preceding stanzas. He merely adds a final comparison, but one that makes his lady equal to all those previously portrayed through "false compare." And to the pointed ambiguity of "she," Shakespeare replies with a personalizing "my love," removing the lady from the dehumanizing shadow of outworn ideals as he turns his parody to positive praise of an altogether earthly mistress.

Sonnets such as this that reflect upon the tradition as a whole find the sonnet myth revived with the characteristic wit of Shakespeare's final turn. But effective as Shakespeare's sonnet poetics may seem to modern eyes—whether it engages in comic mockery or in serious expressions of idealizing love—its most typical qualities were simply not developed by poets in the decades to follow. And this, even though Shakespeare's poetics fully registers a practice in many ways emblematic of his era.

Even more than Petrarch, Shakespeare was able to take metaphysical questions and project them onto an earthly, perceptible plane. In the dramatic relationships of his sonnet protagonists, he humanized, concretized, and thereby intensified the broad concerns with time and love that had occupied the sonnet from its origins. At the same time, the Shakespearean sonnet's witty questioning of language and reference only underscores the tenuous ties established between the elements (linguistic and "real") that the literary sign purports to join.

Many characteristics associated with Shakespeare's *Sonnets* have even been noted in other literary efforts of his and later centuries—but not those written in sonnet form. Kristeva, for instance, notes that between the late Renaissance and the late nineteenth century, the "horizontal" or narrative properties of literature (and she focuses especially on the novel and protonovel) consist of a "metonymic concatenation . . . signifying a progressive creation of metaphors." They reveal oppositional terms that are always "caught up in a network of multiple and always possible deviations . . . giving the illusion of an open structure, impossible to finish, with an arbitrary ending."[48] But, she insists, the sense of the arbitrary remains illusory, framed by thematic "loops" such as life/death, love/hate, fidelity/treason, that ultimately bind the play of meaning.[49]

Though Shakespeare's *Sonnets*—even in their collected form—are not a narrative, they exhibit many of these same traits. With its metonymic concatenation of metaphors, its myriad digressive patterns and partial resolutions, Shakespeare's sequence plays at semantic openness and pursues an ending so arbitrary as to puzzle Shakespeare scholars indefinitely. Still, the openness that his sonnets produce is ultimately bound by the sustained human drama of an "I" and two fully humanized "thou's." From this dramatic structure as well as from the dyadic views of life and death, spirit and flesh, that it molds, the sequence in fact never escapes. On the contrary, it insists upon being seen, explained, and experienced precisely according to these earthly, sensual, and typically humanistic oppositions.

Regardless of Shakespeare's success in forging a powerful new use of the sonnet form, the fact remains that it was not the sonnet genre that would bear his most important legacy. The sonnet, with its strict formal requirements and well-worn conventions, was temporarily unable, for cultural as well as purely poetic reasons, to move further in the direction that Shakespeare had turned it and that his age seemed to demand. Shakespeare's very ability to spark the sonnet sequence with qualities generally associated with other genres helped it to exceed the sixteenth-century limits of the form. But it also suggested that the sonnet, in the context of its own, more limited generic tradition, had reached a sort of impasse.

Perhaps the new emphasis on the separation of self and world that Descartes would open in the seventeenth century, perhaps the new confidence in objective accounts of external nature (reflected in both the empiricist and rationalist philosophies of the time), rendered the characteristically meditative and introspective sonnet suddenly less congenial. Better suited for these new goals were the drama and narrative with their greater scope, flexibility, and authorial distance. Or better, a lyric from outside the old tradition.

Equally important, by the early seventeenth century the Renaissance sonnet's great work had been accomplished, at least in part because its linguistic and political business was done. It had been used to tame what was often regarded as the wild exuberance of medieval vernacular literature and to bring the new developing literatures to greater classical perfection. The youthful vernaculars had used the sonnet for a sort of apprenticeship, to help draw what was needed from the classical and Italianate past. Now they were ready to set off in new and independent directions for which short poetic forms such as the sonnet were not so necessary. Not that the sonnet disappeared completely. It continued to be written by many minor writers, as a relic of the past with little more than a weak, or merely fetishistic, appeal.

Those rare moments when the sonnet was renewed rather than merely rewritten were precisely those in which its rules were powerfully changed to challenge the reader's expectations. The sonnet briefly rediscovered its role as a fragment of a larger whole in Donne's *Holy Sonnets*, though the theme was, of course, religious rather than secular love. Milton, who revised the English sonnet by reviving the grand Italian style (inspired at least in part by the sonnets of Giovanni Della Casa), also underscored its possibilities as an occasional lyric form given to autobiographical or political reflections. But so far did Milton's sonnets generally range from the themes developed in the previous Italian, French, and English tradition that he stood, more often than not, somewhat outside it, the great epic poet remolding the short form to suit his occasional purposes. The case of Shakespeare was different. His themes and form played clearly upon the Petrarchan past, restating its premises in the very act of revising them. The *Sonnets* remained vital heirs to the sonnet tradition. It is simply immediate successors that they lack. The Shakespeare sonnet sequence, with its perplexing ambiguities and powerful human focus, found its true issue in longer forms, such as the drama and the novel, in which some of the same dyadic patterns and complex human situations might work themselves out at greater length and with far fewer restrictions.

The sonnet would not in fact reappear in force until the nineteenth century with poets such as Wordsworth, Keats, Barrett Browning, Alfieri, Foscolo, Gautier, Nerval, and Baudelaire, whose sociopolitical and literary milieux enabled them to restore to the form a distinct purpose, albeit different from that which it had served in the Renaissance. To be sure, the nineteenth century does share some common ground with the Renaissance, and the responsiveness of both periods to the sonnet form is related to a shared belief in the individual self and a certain nostalgia for the literary and historical past. But the role of the artist, the audience to which the sonnet would be addressed, its mode of publication, and the very idea of literary form and expression had changed with the intervening years. And in this very different context, the sonnet seemed to prepare a major reversal, one which would both challenge and revive the tradition that preceded it.

Chapter Three

Referential Irony
The Baudelairean Sonnet

LA VIE ANTÉRIEURE

J'ai longtemps habité sous de vastes portiques
Que les soleils marins teignaient de mille feux,
Et que leurs grands piliers, droits et majestueux,
Rendaient pareils, le soir, aux grottes basaltiques.

Les houles, en roulant les images des cieux,
Mêlaient d'une façon solennelle et mystique
Les tout-puissants accords de leur riche musique
Aux couleurs du couchant reflété par mes yeux.

C'est là que j'ai vécu dans les voluptés calmes,
Au milieu de l'azur, des vagues, des splendeurs
Et des esclaves nus, tout imprégnés d'odeurs,

Qui me rafraîchissaient le front avec des palmes,
Et dont l'unique soin était d'approfondir
Le secret douloureux qui me faisait languir.
—Poem 12[1]

Like a title over a painting, the words "La vie antérieure" invite the reader into a privileged space—outside the everyday, before the present, accessible only through a stretch of the imagination. The persona recalls a life beneath "portiques," touched by the glancing lights of a marine paradise at sunset. "Portiques" already stirs the visual senses, depicting a monumental entrance way and at the same time recalling the ancient painted "portiques" under which Zeno the Pythagorean taught. Framed by this image, a dramatic seascape comes into view, with its rolling waves and plays of sunlight. The sestet changes the focus. Almost like a camera lens, the sonnet turn draws us closer to an observing self, surrounded by exotic nature and by attending slaves. But octave and sestet, evoking first an external, then an internal world, are joined through more than formal contiguity. Both stand at a parallel moment in time; the nature paradise at sunset prefigures the state of the central persona—languishing, at the very point of passage from a "vie antérieure" to the present. The exotic space that the sonnet conjures becomes a temporal metaphor, a space where day meets night, life meets death.

The idyllic splendor of this Baudelairean scene is reflected in a number of other texts of *Les fleurs du mal*. Particularly in the opening section of "Spleen et idéal," sonnets such as "Correspondances" and "Parfum exotique," and odes like "L'Invitation au voyage" and "La chevelure," build the image of a poetic idyll. As the title of Baudelaire's collection suggests, such poems ultimately produce a counterpoint for far less idyllic themes. But the analogical poetics upon which they rest govern *Les fleurs du mal* as a whole. In fact, had Baudelaire ever written his own rhetoric of poetry, he doubtless would have placed the principle of analogy (and its concomitant rhetorical effect, opposition) in the opening chapter. Working on the intersecting levels of verse form, figure, and theme, analogy constitutes a vital element in the "sorcellerie évocatoire" that Baudelaire explicitly seeks to create.[2]

Analogy, with its parallelisms of language and thought, is of course but one expression of the metaphoric principle of equivalence that helps shape every poetic text.[3] And in traditional verse patterns such as those that attracted Baudelaire, the principle of equivalence asserts itself in the measured sequence of syllables, verses, and stanzas as well as in repeated rhyme sounds. But by adding to such formal analogies syntactic and semantic ones, Baudelaire substantially emphasizes the metaphoric principle at work to some degree in all lyric poetry. Indeed, we seldom find Baudelairean sonnets that argue or narrate. Unlike Petrarch's sonnets, with their visible grammar and rationalizing thought sequences, Baudelaire's rely upon resemblances—correspondences that together construct images. And though Baudelaire's persistent emphasis upon imagery may recall Shakespeare's art, his pictures seldom proceed, as Shakespeare's do, in a series of kaleidoscopic transformations. Their analogical plays on language end rather by painting larger canvasses, like the one we see in "La vie antérieure."

In this sonnet, syntax and semantics cooperate to produce meaning through a series of parallelisms. Two moments of first person enunciation—"J'ai longtemps habité sous de vastes portiques" (line 1) and "C'est là que j'ai vécu dans les voluptés calmes" (line 9)—divide the sonnet neatly into two distinct visual perspectives. The parallelism in lyric enunciation is only enhanced by more subtle grammatical parallels framing the sonnet with its outer eight lines. The first four verses, that is, describe "portiques" through a statement (line 1), a complete modifying clause (line 2), a second incomplete modifying clause (line 3), and its object (line 4). Though the last four present a different subject, they rely nonetheless upon an identical syntactic pattern: line 11 stating the theme to be described ("des esclaves nus"), line 12 bringing a complete modifying clause, line 13 an incomplete modifying clause, and line 14 its object. Within this grammatical frame, Baudelaire's image-making words, metaphors, and similes materialize.

Quatrain one gathers three synecdoches—"portiques," "soleils," "feux"—to strike a complex simile ultimately modifying "portiques." Quatrain two presents a personifying metaphor in which the subject "houles" is humanized by a long predicate marked by synesthesia (the sonoral "tout-puissants accords" joins the visual "les couleurs du couchant"). The last six lines rely less on specific figures, more on evocative words—"l'azur," "vagues," "esclaves nus," "odeurs," "palmes"—but build toward a metaphoric substitution in line 14 where there appears the word "secret" rather than a word (such as "maladie") more compatible with "douloureux qui me faisait languir."

So closely woven is the entire sonnet picture that all of its imagery easily folds into the semantic depths of the word "portiques." If, in the octave, the image "portiques" takes its usual meaning of an entrance way or architectural threshold, allowing the persona the vision of a sunset, the sestet builds temporal associations into the spatial threshold at which the persona is poised. Dwelling at this mysterious entrance way and illuminated by the transitional moment of sunset, the self acts as the poem's dying existential center, passing quietly from a life that, as the reader knows, is now "antérieure."

Particularly within one of Baudelaire's most admirably constructed sonnet texts, such carefully worked metaphoric relationships intensify language's intrareferential focus. The poem's course becomes above all a knitting together of its constituent themes and images. It does not ask the reader to consider the codes of the real and the usual, but continually draws him or her into a play of references bounded by the literary artifact. The landscape partakes of the speaker's internal world as the persona's own qualities define themselves against and through the visions described. In the process, both are carried, as it were, to the other side of the everyday, toward what Baudelaire would call the *surnaturel*.

Sonnets such as these carve out a place for a novel sort of *poésie pure* in which the exchange and collusion of linguistic elements with ordinary codes and traditional expectations—collusions so essential to a realistic or incarnational imagery such as that of Shakespeare—are severed in favor of more self-sufficient linguistic structures. Rather than produce a series of reassuring overlaps between poetic language and the everyday language of life or literary tradition, Baudelaire's text emphasizes, even more strongly than did Petrarch's, the difference between his poetic language and life. Still, if Baudelaire's artistry distances his text from our linguistic and semantic expectations, the very fact that he chose to write the way he did reveals a specifically historical purpose as well. As Baudelaire himself was perhaps aware, his sonnet writing in fact signals a minor poetic revolution, and a step toward more recognizably modern themes and style.

By the nineteenth century, the poet's social position—and the very purpose of his poetry—had of course changed enormously from what they had been in the Renaissance, and Baudelaire's particular plight as a nearly destitute art critic and journalist for most of his adult life is a case in point. No longer attached to or supported by a court eager to promote the revival or ornamentation of a national language and literature, the poet of the 1850s was, if anything, a person without a clear social function. Needed neither by an aristocracy nor, as in the Renaissance, by a newly wealthy merchant class seeking to add artistic luster to commercial success, the poet had to appeal now to a growing middle-class public, a reading public broader by far than had ever before existed. Increasingly subjected to the anonymity of industrial work and city life, this was a public in search of new words, new ideas to divert it. It sought entertainment, and the printing press and the rapidly expanding literary journals did bring author and a large and eager reading public well within each other's reach.

In this era of growing industrialization, literature was becoming, in short, a product like any other. This was as clear in the case of the sonnet as of any other literary form, for the sonnet found an easy commercial outlet in small journals and newspapers. It is not surprising that, under such changed circumstances, the very conception of the form changed. The sonnet's graphic potential, its quality as a written entity, acquired an importance it had never had before. Wordsworth, for instance, spoke of the sonnet as an "orbicular" form, and a new concern with the "image" and the "symbol" drew attention to the imaginative space that a sonnet could create.[4] Thematically, the sonnet began to draw the image of a poet-writer, rather than a speaker or singer. As the poetic self came to be portrayed more routinely as a writer rather than a singer, the sonnet's capacity to depict the lyric subject seemed only to grow. It may, in fact, have been the sonnet's reassertion of its traditional gift for capturing the changefulness of an "inner self" that best accounts for the new impetus that it experienced in the mid-nineteenth century.

By the 1800s, the empirical directions of eighteenth-century thought had already pointed to a new appreciation of individual feeling, and more idealistic trends developing through Kant and eventually Hegel had helped to bring the notion of self, especially the inner worth of the individual as a spiritual being, to central importance. The lyric found itself cast once more at the center of literary experience as the genre most apt for conveying introspective statements; and among lyric forms the sonnet once again interested poets, this time less because it offered a classical literary exercise than because of its brevity and its set of multiple closures that lent themselves particularly well to glimpses of the human spirit. But the sonnet, of course, also came to Romantic poets charged with an illustrious tradition to which at least some responded strongly, if also very differently, depending upon their individual time, place, and poetic inclination.

The intensely nationalistic nineteenth century did play to some extent on what might be called the patriotic dimension of the sonnet. It became a vehicle for reaching back, not only to the classical tradition but to what was by now an impressive national past. It could establish a certain continuity with the very beginning of vernacular poetry, and did so with special grace in the hands of the English poets Wordsworth, Coleridge, and Keats. Keats's sonnets, which take up first the Italian and then the English form, while adding vivid imagery and sensorial detail evocative of the Shakespearean text, best epitomize the happy transition of the sonnet into a distinctly native Romantic form.

But in France, where traditional continuities of all sorts had been broken by a jagged series of revolutions, the sonnet was not so smoothly situated for popularity. It was plagued, in part, by associations with disfavored courtly life and even more by concomitant associations with an outmoded, stylized, and rhetorical poetry.[5] During the late eighteenth century and the beginning of the nineteenth, the sonnet was in fact scarcely cultivated. Moreover, for reasons of personal temperament, the greatest poet of the age, Victor Hugo, avoided the form almost completely. His expansive genius turned instead to larger canvasses in which self and world could fuse. Speaking in grand symbolic gestures and through much looser lyric forms, sometimes hundreds of lines long, Hugo's poetic enterprises inevitably dwarfed the early sonnet writing of Sainte-Beuve, Gautier, Musset, Nerval, and that of Baudelaire's own literary circle.[6]

Placed at the liminal moment between Romanticism and what would be known to us as modernity, Baudelaire's particular use of the sonnet offered a strange and, at that time, surprising, amalgam. While rejecting the sonnet's traditional reflections on nature in favor of a more idiosyncratic and more urban world, his poetry exuded a keen awareness of the sonnet's classical past. Not only did he allow earlier poets to speak with clarity through his own lyrics (usually to better illustrate his own poetic difference), he retained a healthy respect for the institution of rhetoric long and by then unfavorably associated with fixed verse forms. In Baudelaire's eyes, the rhetorical tradition did not so much impose binding external rules as reveal universal psychological norms. "It is evident," he wrote, "that rhetoric and prosody are not an arbitrarily invented tyranny but a collection of rules demanded by the organization of the spiritual being."[7] It may indeed be that Baudelaire took his great interest in already old-fashioned verse forms, and in the sonnet in particular, in part because he believed that rhetorical form reflects an inner state, an unconscious world.

The seriousness with which Baudelaire approached the sonnet form showed up in the finished product. In a general way, he accepted the sonnet's traditional prosody, maintaining the standard bipartite structure of the French form that had come down to him from the Renaissance. But just as clearly he modified, even revolutionized, the particulars of the rhyme scheme to produce unique reflections of this or that moment of artistic feeling and thought. (Counting up Baudelaire's thirty-two original rhyme schemes, Henri Morier, in his *Dictionnaire de poétique et de rhétorique*, even goes so far as to call these many variations on the classical French form "faux sonnets.")[8] At the same time, the poet's use of titles for his sonnets, part of a heavier accent on visual form, denoted a poetics of inscription rather than speech.

But what is most remarkable in Baudelaire's use of the sonnet is how he introduced a past literary tradition only, it seems, to undermine it. Nothing was more shaken by these literary tactics than the very hallmark of the sonnet tradition from Petrarch to the nineteenth century, namely the quest for a powerful and, if possible, an integral self. For although the poetry of the early nineteenth century in France (and Hugo remains the most imposing example) had brought novelty to the lyric tradition, it had for the most part reinforced those elements of self-contemplation and almost mystic correspondence between self and world, humanity and history, that had been central to the sonnet tradition from its Italian beginnings.[9] But the 1850s were years when a sense of nature, of historical continuity, and of self-possession began to be threatened by the disjunctive, impersonal tempo of modern city life. And the sonnets of *Les fleurs du mal* reveal, perhaps better than any literary text of the period, a concomitant breaking point in the lyric tradition. What could be mistaken from Baudelaire's metaphorical sonnet form alone as a clear revival of an older sonnet tradition amounted in fact to a revolutionary vision of an unstable world and a disunified, curiously de-personalized self, a vision that, to an important extent, augured yet further lyric transformations. And it is by his rhetoric as well as his themes that Baudelaire accomplished so much.

ALLEGORY, IRONY, AND POÉSIE PURE

The rhetorical means to Baudelaire's change of lyric pace are specific, and specifically directed against the mimetic and symbolic practice common in the Romantic poetry of his day. Instead of a reliance upon the poetic symbol, with its tendency to project a sense of totality between speaker and world, between language and experience;[10] instead of the collusions of sense producing a mimetic realism, Baudelaire more often than not uses his highly metaphoric sonnet structure to underscore difference and alienation. For the metaphoric, in its patterns of similarity and difference rather than contiguity, lends itself to strategies quite at odds with the incarnational poetics of Shakespeare. In Baudelaire's hands, the metaphoric turns instead to allegory and irony.

The intimate relationship between allegory and irony has long been acknowledged by the rhetorical tradition. Allegory, in its literal Greek sense, means "speaking otherwise than one seems to speak," and if the term now characterizes a quite extraordinary variety of literary statement, it inevitably implies a doubleness of meaning: the verbal picture and the idea, or the narrative and its meaning. It is precisely this persistent analogous doubling, this marked separation of language from what it purports to describe, that allows allegory to take its stand in opposition to the symbolic and the mimetic, and to the multiple collusions on which they rest. At the same time, allegory's typical doubleness brings it particularly close to irony.

Irony, defined since Aristotle's day as "saying one thing and meaning another," similarly acquires its effect by the difference it traces between a meaning directly expressed and an opposite meaning intended by the author and understood by the reader. One modern rhetorician has even remarked that "irony is clearly a particular, 180 degree reversed instance of allegory's double meaning. . . . The ironist depends on an allegorical habit of mind in his reader, a habit that will juxtapose surface and real meaning."[11]

In a study of the two modes that touch Baudelaire more closely, Paul De Man describes allegory and irony as interrelated devices.[12] But referring to Baudelaire's essay, "De l'essence du rire," as well as a variety of English and German texts, he offers an explanation of the distinctions between the two. He describes, for instance, two underlying characteristics of irony. Most important, irony depends upon an intrasubjective experience, a distinctive doubleness in the speaking subject. Baudelaire provides the reference here: "[L]a puissance du rire est dans le rieur et nullement dans l'objet du rire. Ce n'est point l'homme qui tombe qui rit de sa propre chute, à moins qu'il ne soit un philosophe, un homme qui ait acquis, par habitude, la force de se dédoubler rapidement et d'assister comme spectateur désintéressé aux phénomènes de son *moi*."[13] Secondly, De Man points out, irony achieves its effect through the sense of simultaneity that it evokes: "Irony is instantaneous like an 'explosion' and the fall is sudden. . . . Two selves, the empirical as well as the ironic, are simultaneously present, juxtaposed within the same moment but as two irreconcilable and disjointed beings.... The difference now resides in the subject whereas time is reduced to one single moment."[14]

Allegory would work somewhat differently. It consists in a textual rather than subjective doubling—a reference from one poetic sign to another earlier one. It tends, moreover, to stretch out in narrative time rather than condense into a single, simultaneous vision of a fall.[15] But allegory ultimately joins the ironic in its demystifying mission, working against both the organicism that the Romantic symbol portrays and the mimesis in which fiction and reality seem to coincide. Both succeed in using language to wrench us from the illusory correspondence between self and world, to assert the specifically fictional status of language and, in the process, to deny any comforting sense of eternity that such close identification between self and world, language and representation, promises. They point instead to the temporal void that might be viewed, at least for the modern, as the human lot.[16]

Helpful though it is, De Man's discussion, clearly aiming at general conclusions about post-Romantic rhetorical modes rather than the explanation of any single poet's strategy, would have to be somewhat qualified to reflect the particulars of Baudelaire's sonnet poetics. Although one might use De Man's distinctions to characterize the Baudelairean sonnet as a basically ironic mode—founded upon a keen sense of simultaneity and a continual, highly disconcerting self-speculation—one would have to reemphasize the flexibility Baudelaire in fact attributes to the ironic and underscore the supportive role that allegory frequently plays within it.

For instance, Baudelaire makes plain that a higher form of irony, which he calls the "comique absolu" or the "grotesque," has the power to reach toward something more profound, more innocent, than the usual sense of irony would suggest: "[L]e rire causé par le grotesque a en soi quelque chose de profond, d'axiomatique et de primitif qui se rapproche beaucoup plus de la vie innocente et de la joie absolue que le rire causé par le comique de moeurs."[17] Baudelaire elsewhere describes this truly innocent sort of poetry that seems to leave the ironic completely behind: "[S]i dans ces mêmes nations ultracivilisées, une intelligence, poussée par une ambition supérieure, veut franchir les limites de l'orgueil mondain et s'élancer hardiment vers la poésie pure, dans cette poésie, limpide et profonde comme la nature, le rire fera défaut comme dans l'âme du Sage."[18] An "innocent" poetry, hovering between the grotesque and the expression of joy, is, as we shall see, a common feature of Baudelaire's sonnets. In fact, one can describe his sonnet strategies as ironic only if one bears in mind this particular ironic frontier and if one admits its close relationship to Baudelairean allegory. For, carefully considered, both rhetorical norms participate in a single Baudelairean view of self and of art.

As Baudelaire himself states in the same essay on laughter, the power of irony—be it the "comique significatif" with its intersubjective humor, or the "comique absolu" with the distance it places between self and a nonhuman world—is in fact but a particular expression of a more general artistic phenomenon. It belongs "dans la classe de tous les phénomènes artistiques qui dénotent dans l'être humain l'existence *d'une dualité permanente, la puissance d'être à la fois soi et un autre*" (emphasis added).[19] If we can judge from Baudelaire's critical comments elsewhere as well as from his sonnet poetics, the themes, if not the structure, of his allegory belong precisely in this same self-reflexive class.

Even though Baudelairean allegory generally works by the principle that De Man has stated—it refers to an earlier textual sign either within the single literary artifact or in an earlier work, and thus depends upon a necessary anteriority of meaning—its most distinctive feature is that it tends to offer in the end little more than universalizations, objective pictures of a situation or a state of the speaking self. What is more, although Baudelairean allegory may well take on a narrative drive—and does so, I would argue, nowhere more effectively than in the overall structure of *Les fleurs du mal* itself—this is neither its only nor even its usual form. In short poems such as the sonnet, allegory generally takes a more time-limited structure, finding its most evident linguistic expression in the frequent capitalizations that haunt the Baudelairean text with their suggestions of universal beings: le Temps, la Débauche, la Mort, la Haine, l'Amour, la Vie, l'Art. And precisely such allegorical figures as these help produce a sense of "une dualité permanente," the self-doubling most closely associated with ironic themes. It is, in fact, allegory's power to mirror the self that Baudelaire notes in the course of "Le poème du haschisch," in one of his most elaborate statements on the figure:

> [N]ous noterons, en passant, que l'allégorie, ce genre si *spirituel*, que les peintres maladroits nous ont accoutumés à mépriser, mais qui est vraiment l'une des formes primitives et les plus naturelles de la poésie, reprend sa domination légitime dans l'intelligence illuminée par l'ivresse. . . . Paysages dentelés, horizons fuyants, perspectives de villes blanchies par la lividité cadavéreuse de l'orage ou illuminées par les ardeurs concentrées des soleils couchants,— profondeur de l'espace, allégorie de la profondeur du temps,—la danse, le geste ou la déclamation des comédiens, si vous vous êtes jeté dans un théâtre,—la première phrase venue, si vos yeux tombent sur un livre,—tout enfin, l'universalité des êtres se dresse devant vous avec une gloire nouvelle non soupçonnée jusqu'alors. . . . La musique . . . vous parle de vous-même et vous raconte le poëme de votre vie: elle s'incorpore à vous, et vous vous fondez en elle.[20]

And indeed the Baudelairean sonnet often uses strands of allegorical self-reflection to weave its irony—be it through reference to another human being (as in "Sonnet d'automne"), an effect of the grotesque (as in "Spleen"), or something nearer to a paradisal innocence (as in "La vie antérieure"). Allegory only intensifies the sonnet's self-reflection and the ironic abyss of self-mirroring in which these sonnets so often conclude. Both join to point toward the curious doubling that acts as source and product of literally all Baudelaire's rhetorical figures.

In these often disconcerting auto-reflections, the thematic effects of Baudelaire's allegory are thus not at all the traditional sort. They only underscore the revolutionary character of his sonnet statements. If, since Dante, allegory had been used for the most part to give self—and natural world—a place in a larger eternal or human plan, Baudelaire uses it to move in a contrary direction. It tends to work against any sense of stability, against an established hierarchy of persons, things, beliefs, against the very sense of a secure place for the self. Marked by a strange interchangeability between internal and external images, physical and spiritual portraits, self and what appears to be other, Baudelairean allegory seems only to intensify the theme of a veritable abyss of self-reflection, the unsettling continuity of self-speculation that intrudes even upon Baudelaire's most apparently serene, most paradisal poems. Moreover, the anteriority, the flight of meaning from one sign to another that De Man points out, generally becomes, in Baudelaire's hands, but part and parcel of a painful ironic shuttle with no apparent beginning and no foreseeable end.

At times this complex interplay achieves its effect through the different linguistic levels at which the Baudelairean text performs. As in many allegorical statements, Baudelaire's allegories make their self-referential meaning largely through tropes, the more purely cognitive level of the poem, the one most given to reference and meaning. His irony, on the other hand, leaves its mark most clearly on the poetic enunciation, the performative level of the text, that most easily reveals a pervasive and simultaneous doubling within the subject, one occurring at the very moment of speech.

"La vie antérieure" is a case in point. Its figures and tropes evoke an exotic world based in part on Baudelaire's youthful voyage to the West Indies, on his readings of specific literary texts (works of Laforgue and Poe come to mind), perhaps on hearing *Lohengrin*.[21] But at least part of his inspiration derived from the well-known Romantic *topos* of an earthly paradise. Rousseau, for one, stands in the background, as the best-known source of the Romantic paradise. But perhaps for Baudelaire's "La vie antérieure," Victor Hugo was a more specific reference, particularly in poems such as "Que la musique date du seizième siècle" (*Les rayons et les ombres*).

On the one hand, it is to such texts as these (and the larger tradition to which they themselves refer) that Baudelaire's poem seems to point and toward this tradition that the signs of his own poem immediately escape, as if toward some happier anteriority. On the other hand, the beginning to end course of this typically

The Baudelairean Sonnet / 105

structured sonnet reveals its own intrareferentiality as it brings this paradisal vision to bear specifically on the portrait of a poetic self. As we have seen, the sonnet's analogical structure, complete with its syntactic and figural correspondences, bonds octave to sestet, external world to observing persona. Through a series of reflections between the sunset of an earthly paradise and the persona's own individual passage from "La vie antérieure," the Baudelairean allegory takes shape as a well-molded circuit of sense.

But if the sonnet imagery and the figures on which it depends thus work to allegorize, to universalize a moment in the observer's past, its enunciation engulfs the whole in a further, grammatical self-doubling. Beginning in line 1, the present moment of speech marks its distance from a past already experienced—"J'ai . . . habité"—a distance only reinforced by line 9's "j'ai vécu." The self about to "fall" from an idyllic "vie antérieure" is observed through the memorializing eyes of a second ironic self, present, detached, and speculative. Beautiful and comforting though it is, the idyllic world is nonetheless gone, and the entire poem plays out its meaning in the restricted space of a divided and aware self.

It is precisely in such textually unified sonnets, using allegorical identifications to support the sense of a fall, that Baudelaire's "pure poetry" acquires its distinctive, differential touch. It is also in this way that difference becomes an historical position, marking the gap between a peculiarly modern temperament and all that came before. In fact, considered from the viewpoint of Baudelaire's keen awareness of his own human and poetic place (suggested not only in poetry but also in prose works such as "Le peintre de la vie moderne")[22] no poem better portrays Baudelaire's historical posture than "La vie antérieure." Poised at the very portico, the brink of the modern, the poet witnesses the birth of a new moment, painfully conscious of an irreparable rift in time, whose most telling mark is a pronounced self-alienation.

If we take Walter Benjamin's term "aura" to mean, above all, the presence of historical, even ritualistic, roots in a tradition of individual craftsmanship and "original" works,[23] it is precisely this quality that Baudelaire has to acknowledge as forever lost. In the era of photography, of Haussmann's boulevards and a growing quantity of newspapers, leaflets, and literary journals, it was only too evident that a rapidly changing technology had vastly altered traditional patterns of life. And temporal cleavages that stem from the breaking of vital continuities mark every page of *Les fleurs du mal*.

The very use of short fixed verse forms such as the sonnet defeats Romantic expectations of a freer, more fluid, more expressive lyric. It makes reading the collection an experience in halting, differential movements, brief surprising flashes of imagery surrounded by darkness and quiet. The internal structure of Baudelaire's sonnets only accentuates this jarring effect by using trope and syntax to work against the traditional grain of linguistic time. Sonnet after sonnet finds him transforming linguistic time, which could make for narrative and logical development, into a static but disquieting space.

More than one piece of his prose reveals Baudelaire's general fascination with the pictorial allegorization of the temporal. In "Richard Wagner et *Tannhäuser* à Paris," the opening pages bear precisely upon music's power to prompt a visual response in the listener's mind:

> Je me souviens que, dès les premières mesures, je subis une de ces impressions heureuses que presque tous les hommes imaginatifs ont connues, par le rêve, dans le sommeil. . . . Ensuite je me peignis involontairement l'état délicieux d'un homme en proie à une grande rêverie dans une solitude absolue, mais une solitude avec *un immense horizon* et une *large lumière diffuse; l'immensité* sans autre décor qu'elle-même. Bientôt j'éprouvai la sensation d'une *clarté* plus vive,

> *d'une intensité de lumière* croissant avec une telle rapidité, que les nuances fournies par le dictionnaire ne suffiraient pas à exprimer *ce surcroît toujours renaissant d'ardeur et de blancheur*. Alors je conçus pleinement l'idée d'une âme se mouvant dans un milieu lumineux, d'une extase *faite de volupté et de connaissance*, et planant au-dessus et bien loin du monde naturel.[24]

The transformation of time into imaginative space is at least as marked in Baudelaire's poetry as in this piece of music criticism. In fact, after considering Baudelaire's some sixty sonnets, the most frequently appearing form in *Les fleurs du mal* (taking up almost half of the 1861 edition), one can only conclude that if the poet is a master at manipulating effects of sound and sequence, and at exerting the powers of lexical ambiguity, he invariably opts for linguistic effects that guarantee a strong spatial impression. These are, as Pound would say, "phanopoetic" in their ability to "cast images upon the visual imagination."[25]

It is typically by repetitions and parallelisms that Baudelaire achieves his pictorial effects. Be it through successive tropes or through figures of syntax, he strives to transform the forward drive of language into the simultaneity of the image and, in the process, creates a static moment particularly susceptible to the "fall" of Baudelairean irony. Considered diagrammatically, his rhetoric, like Shakespeare's, would entail a primarily vertical axis to reflect the highly paradigmatic or associative effect of his poetry. But as Baudelaire's sonnets move through the repetitive patterns formed by syntax and figure, they present not so much a chain of contrasting images as an imaginative space oriented around a single developing vision. The changeful, progressive time of language gives way to an imaginatively perceptible, highly unified space:

	lyric space
paradigmatic	Irony
(reader's imagination)	Allegory
	Synesthesia
	Metaphor

	Personification
	Comparison
	Assonance
syntagmatic	Alliteration
(vision of the text)	Anaphora
	―――――――――
	linear movement of visible syntagm

Such imagistic translations of time often build allegorically, only to lend themselves to Baudelaire's ironic disruptions. At other moments, they conjure idyllic escapes whose very artifice marks their difference from an earlier tradition. Either way, syntax and tropes cooperate to produce thematically self-reflexive meditations. A series of tropes based on analogy lends "La musique," for instance, a peculiarly spatial quality, making of it a virtual picture of music:

LA MUSIQUE

La musique souvent me prend comme une mer!
    Vers ma pâle étoile,
Sous un plafond de brume ou dans un vaste éther,
    Je mets à la voile;
La poitrine en avant et les poumons gonflés
    Comme de la toile,
J'escalade le dos des flots amoncelès
    Que la nuit me voile;

Je sens vibrer en moi toutes les passions
    D'un vaisseau qui souffre;
Le bon vent, la tempête et ses convulsions
    Sur l'immense gouffre
Me bercent. D'autres fois, calme plat, grand miroir
    De mon désespoir!

For his visual effect, Baudelaire here relies upon a combination of figures—simile, metaphor, and what might be called identification—all common enough in the Baudelairean repertoire and easily marshalled to create large spatial effects. In "La musique," as in the collection as a whole, the simile is perhaps the most highly prized of the three. Introduced by "comme" or "ainsi," and therefore resting upon the explicit intervention of the poet's voice, simile disrupts usual verbal meanings far less dramatically than metaphor. Left semantically intact, words like "mer" and "musique" work their associative overlaps of sense only retrospectively, at the end of the simile, and then only if the reader gives his or her intellectual assent.

Not so, of course, with metaphor. More covert in structure, a metaphor such as "J'escalade le dos des flots amoncelés" defies the reader's intellectual scrutiny. In place of a logical conjunction, it relies on the less easily refuted logic of syntax, to which the reader almost automatically responds and behind which the poetic persona can hide his governing hand. With no overt comparison between self and ship—the "vaisseau" does not appear in the sonnet's syntax—the sense of the passage comes from the largely unconscious process of reconciling subject and predicate. Inevitably, the image such figures create is a more private affair than arises out of the simile. Here this associative collision of sense has the effect of violating the usual verbal compartmentalizations of meaning. The world appears profoundly new.

Curiously, for all their ability to escape from the common code of accepted meanings, Baudelaire's metaphors seldom become obscure. As in the sonnet "La musique," the poet usually prepares the way for his metaphors through a series of similes and identifications. Figures such as "je sens vibrer en moi toutes les passions / D'un vaisseau qui souffre," for instance, place both overlapping terms—here "je" and "vaisseau"—directly in the sonnet syntax.[26] The text builds gradually from similes at the beginnings of both quatrains, and from an identification at the sonnet turn, to metaphor proper. All cooperate in producing a single picture in which self is ship, and music the sea.

Only in the final line is the metaphoric buildup deflated through a swift ironic reversal. To the "calme plat," perfectly acceptable on the metaphoric level of the text, Baudelaire juxtaposes a direct "de-figured" reference to the speaking self. The five final syllables—"De mon désespoir"—suddenly project a fully human self, expressing "real" human passions rather than metaphorical nautical actions. The poem's allegory of escape, based upon the analogy between self and ship, music and sea, founders in a final ironic self-reference in which the persona details his distance from the imagery out of which he seems to be made. Abruptly then, the sonnet picture, so carefully drawn in the course of the preceding lines, claims its character of pure fiction, admits to being a mere temporary escape from the real and from the self.

Although analogical tropes such as those of "La musique" create some of Baudelaire's most memorable sonnets, among them "Correspondances," "La beauté," "Avec ses vêtements," and "La fontaine de sang," the poet turns just as often to other techniques. If a sonnet such as "Le flambeau vivant" does not take music as its theme, it does stop the flow of linguistic time in a particularly arresting picture. Here the strategy is largely syntactical, tending less to effect a fall than simply to convey the fictional estrangement typical of Baudelaire's sonnet idylls:

LE FLAMBEAU VIVANT

Ils marchent devant moi, ces Yeux pleins de lumières,
Qu'un Ange très-savant a sans doute aimantés;
Ils marchent, ces divins frères qui sont mes frères,
Secouant dans mes yeux leurs feux diamantés.

Me sauvant de tout piège et de tout péché grave,
Ils conduisent mes pas dans la route du Beau;
Ils sont mes serviteurs et je suis leur esclave;
Tout mon être obéit à ce vivant flambeau.

Charmants Yeux, vous brillez de la clarté mystique
Qu'ont les cierges brûlant en plein jour; le soleil
Rougit, mais n'éteint pas leur flamme fantastique;

Ils célèbrent la Mort, vous chantez le Réveil;
Vous marchez en chantant le réveil de mon âme,
Astres dont nul soleil ne peut flétrir la flamme!

While the sonnet is replete with lexical repetitions—nine words, not counting pronouns and prepositions, occur at least twice in the text—each finds its place in a singularly repetitious, even anaphoric syntax. The pronoun "ils" begins four of the initial eight lines and even echoes at the beginning of tercet two. Such repetitions provide a graphic—and phonic—unity that is only reinforced semantically. For anaphora, in its linguistic sense of "a segment of discourse the meaning of which may be derived only from another segment of the same discourse,"[27] also plays its part in building Baudelaire's intrareferential imagery.

The classic example of the anaphoric word is the pronoun, for its function is precisely one of re-presenting a meaning whose reference is already, or soon, to be given. If in a spoken message, a physical gesture may well supply the meaning of a pronoun, in a poem it is surrounding signs that usually do so. Baudelaire, along with many later poets, sometimes chooses to leave such re-presenting references imprecise and thereby insulate his meaning in mystery. More often, he employs anaphoric pronouns to underscore—without fully insulating—the highly individualized fiction that his texts create.

In "Le flambeau vivant," anaphoric patterning intensifies and estranges the quite conventional sonnet theme of the loved one's shining eyes leading to spiritual salvation. A semantically void "ils," accompanied by its humanizing predicate "marchent," at the beginning of line 1, produces an immediate personification of the eyes. Humanized, masculinized, and seemingly detached from any particular person or thing, the eyes take on a divine quality as the pronoun "que" anaphorically confers on them mystic powers—"Qu'un Ange très-savant a sans doute aimantés"—and the apposition of line 3 labels them specifically "divins frères." Thanks to this play of opposition, the pronoun "ils" easily supports the second quatrain's initial participial phrase, making moral agents of seemingly autonomous, divinized beings.

Relying upon the same anaphoric strategy, the sestet takes a further leap into the marvelous. The eyes bear first the "clarté mystique" and then the "flamme fantastique" of ecclesiastical candles, rivaling the sun with their mystic light. Finally—"Astres dont nul soleil ne peut flétrir la flamme!"—they transcend the human altogether.

A carefully gauged intrareferentiality thus estranges the "eyes" from reference to the loved woman and eventually from all that is human. But though the sonnet's metaphors escalate slowly and with characteristic preparation to their mystical finale, theirs is not an imagery that the reader can accept passively. As in the sonnet "La musique," the sestet of "Le flambeau vivant" produces its ironic effects. True, it is not a matter of deflating previous imagery in a final ironic reversal. Rather, it is a matter of turning on one's own poetic strategy precisely in order to underscore its artifice. And it is no less disturbing, for in a sonnet whose "surnaturalisme" rests essentially upon its anaphoric patterns, Baudelaire has suddenly interjected a disconcerting play of pronouns. "Vous" in line 9, for example, surprises the reader with an unprepared reference to the shining eyes, only to be followed by the equally unexpected reference of "ils" to religious candles. To make matters yet more complex, "ils" is placed in opposition to "vous"; the candles celebrate death while the eyes bring new life. Though the technique is different, and a good deal more subtle than that of "La musique," the end of this sonnet, like that of the other, troubles the picture that has been carefully built with the sonnet's unfolding. Its anaphoric structure suggests a refusal of fixed reference, and escapes not only from a firm grounding in conventional codes, but even from a stable grammatical framework. In so doing, the sonnet produces its strange, alienating effect.

Poems such as "La musique" and "Le flambeau vivant" show Baudelaire's uncanny capacity to highlight the lyric as imaginative space. These disquieting halts in the pace of lyric time, traceable at least in part to the poet's pictorial rhetoric, are only reinforced at other levels of the reader's experience. Discontinuities also arise in the vertical or associative dimension that each text—and the collection as a whole—sets up with the preceding lyric tradition. Merely by emphasizing the fictional status of his poems, Baudelaire already sets them against the more realistic modes that he particularly scorned. But in turning so frequently to the sonnet, he can dramatize his departure from centuries-old conventions.

Purely in terms of form, Baudelaire strikes some significant changes. Entirely capable of managing the classical French sonnet pattern with its octave and sestet punctuated by an internal couplet—ABBA, ABBA, CCD, EED—Baudelaire in fact chose this form for only six of his sonnets. The rest retain just enough of the standard rhyme scheme to be recognizable as sonnets, but revise octave, sestet and, not infrequently, line length, to produce a range of distinct and thoroughly unpredictable patterns. Baudelaire thus evokes the traditional sonnet form while systematically signaling his detachment from it.

This determined break with a traditional past figures more subtly, but no less pervasively, in Baudelaire's treatment of the sonnet's conventional Renaissance themes. Looking back to the poets of the French Pléiade (and perhaps to the larger Italian and English tradition that influenced them), Baudelaire drew new and energetic lines of his own. Often, his novelty comes through quite directly. Take, for example, the well-worked theme of death. In the earlier Renaissance tradition that Baudelaire's very use of the sonnet was bound to evoke, the theme was generally graced with some hope and expectation—whether of divine immortality (as in Petrarch's "Volo con l'ali de' pensieri al cielo," sonnet 362), or the more limited immortality promised by beautifully wrought tombs or verses (as in Shakespeare's "Devouring Time, blunt thou the lion's paws"), or of a final reunion with mother earth (as in the ode "De l'élection de son sépulchre" of Ronsard). But as the sonnet "Le mort joyeux" suggests, for Baudelaire death seems to bring only the certitude of continued torture, of a further disintegration of self, or perhaps the pretext for a grotesque literary prank:

LE MORT JOYEUX

Dans une terre grasse et pleine d'escargots
Je veux creuser moi-même une fosse profonde,
Où je puisse à loisir étaler mes vieux os
Et dormir dans l'oubli comme un requin dans l'onde.

Je hais les testaments et je hais les tombeaux;
Plutôt que d'implorer une larme du monde,
Vivant, j'aimerais mieux inviter les corbeaux
A saigner tous les bouts de ma carcasse immonde.

> O vers! noirs compagnons sans oreille et sans yeux,
> Voyez venir à vous un mort libre et joyeux;
> Philosophes viveurs, fils de la pourriture,
>
> A travers ma ruine allez donc sans remords,
> Et dites-moi s'il est encor quelque torture,
> Pour ce vieux corps sans âme et mort parmi les morts!

The sonnet produces its effect precisely through a parodic inversion of traditional themes. The poet has already lost the soul that would grant divine immortality (line 14); he scorns testaments and tombs (line 5). And though he emphasizes the generative cycles of nature through references to the symbolic spiral of the "escargot" in line 1, and to water and marine life in lines 3 and 4, all that the force of nature really seems to promise is the final decomposition that physical death brings to an already dead soul. And nothing reveals the parody more forcefully than the ironic relationship of the sonnet's title to its closing lines.[28]

Equally revealing is Baudelaire's revision of standard courtly love themes, which he confronts either with a simple exaggeration of the tradition's most overt Platonizing tendencies or, more frequently, with an imaging of physical eroticism clearly contrary to the idealized Renaissance portrait of the lady. As already noted, "Le flambeau vivant" itself offers a good example of Baudelaire's ability to play upon the theme of a spiritualized beloved and the beneficence of her glance. Here, as in a few other of his love poems, and particularly in "Je t'adore à l'égale de la voûte nocturne," Baudelaire draws out to the extreme the conventional distance from the beloved. In so doing, he minimizes—perhaps even more than did Petrarch, Shakespeare, or the versatile Ronsard—the importance of the loved one, as he subsumes her presence to a series of mysterious metaphors.[29]

But it was Baudelaire's powerful imaging of the erotic that earned him immediate renown as it simultaneously invited the censoring of several important pieces published in the first, 1857 edition of *Les fleurs du mal*. One of the censored texts, "Les bijoux," was apparently composed about 1842 for Marie Daubrun. Though not written in sonnet form, its eight-quatrain design with its turn in meaning after line 24 suggests an expansion of the sonnet form, as if Baudelaire wished to "write large" his daring departure from previous idealizing conventions.

LES BIJOUX

La très-chère était nue, et, connaissant mon coeur,
Elle n'avait gardé que ses bijoux sonores,
Dont le riche attirail lui donnait l'air vainqueur
Qu'ont dans leurs jours heureux les esclaves des Mores.

Quand il jette en dansant son bruit vif et moqueur,
Ce monde rayonnant de métal et de pierre
Me ravit en extase, et j'aime à la fureur
Les choses où le son se mêle à la lumière.

Elle était donc couchée et se laissait aimer,
Et du haut du divan elle souriait d'aise
A mon amour profond et doux comme la mer,
Qui vers elle montait comme vers sa falaise.

Les yeux fixés sur moi, comme un tigre domptée,
D'un air vague et rêveur elle essayait des poses,
Et la candeur unie à la lubricité
Donnait un charme neuf à ses métamorphoses;

Et son bras et sa jambe, et sa cuisse et ses reins,
Polis comme de l'huile, onduleux comme un cygne,
Passaient devant mes yeux clairvoyants et sereins;
Et son ventre et ses seins, ces grappes de ma vigne,

S'avançaient, plus calins que les Anges du mal,
Pour troubler le repos où mon âme était mise,
Et pour la déranger du rocher de cristal
Où, calme et solitaire, elle s'était assise.

Je croyais voir unis par un nouveau dessin
Les hanches de l'Antiope au buste d'un imberbe,
Tant sa taille faisait ressortir son bassin.
Sur ce teint fauve et brun, le fard était superbe!

> —Et la lampe s'étant résignée à mourir,
> Comme le foyer seul illuminait la chambre,
> Chaque fois qu'il poussait un flamboyant soupir,
> Il inondait de sang cette peau couleur d'ambre!

Here, Baudelaire proposes a series of sexual motifs seldom so frankly approached in the Renaissance tradition: the nudity of the woman before her lover, her erotic posing to arouse his desire, the intimate setting suggested by the "divan." Not that Baudelaire abandons the standard Petrarchan conventions altogether. In several respects, his imagery spells a metamorphosis rather than a rejection of standard courtly love themes. The lover's passive contemplation of his loved one, for instance, traces the familiar stance of the servant-lover. And the fetishistic attention that the Petrarchan tradition lavishes on the woman's hair, breast, arm, hand, or glove seems merely to change its focus here—to the glint of jewels on the naked body, the color of cosmetics or lamplight on beautiful skin. As in Petrarch's *Rime sparse*, this concentration on particulars results in the Renaissance motif of the fragmentation of the beloved.

But precisely through Petrarchan resonance, Baudelaire strikes a novel note, one deriving not only from his more overt, more modern expression of sexual love but from the way the poet resolves sensuality into well-drawn images of plastic art. If Petrarch's Laura was shaped out of a highly traditional set of courtly love, nature, or mythic allusions and Shakespeare's dark mistress out of a parody of the same, the mistress of the Baudelairean text generally arises out of metaphors newly attentive to the human senses and, as we have seen, singularly able to awaken the imaginative space of the reader's mind. The turn of this thirty-two-line poem is a case in point. Here, the sensual imagery of the first twenty-four lines resolves in the poet's vision of a work of art:

> Je croyais voir unis par un nouveau dessin
> Les hanches de l'Antiope au buste d'un imberbe,
> Tant sa taille faisait ressortir son bassin.
> Sur ce teint fauve et brun, le fard était superbe!

> —Et la lampe s'étant résignée à mourir,
> Comme le foyer seul illuminait la chambre,
> Chaque fois qu'il poussait un flamboyant soupir,
> Il inondait de sang cette peau couleur d'ambre!

Such Baudelairean metamorphoses of desired mistress into artistic matter recur in sonnet form as well—in "Parfum exotique," for instance, in which the perfume of the mistress' hair leads to a poetic reverie eclipsing the woman in an exotic landscape. Even more dramatically, the four-sonnet sequence, "Un fantome," transposes eroticism into rapt contemplation of a distanced object. If the poet is drawn as a painter in the first sonnet, in the third sonnet, entitled, "Le cadre," he paints his mistress and the jewels that frame her in a striking evocation of "Les bijoux":

III

LE CADRE

> Comme un beau cadre ajoute à la peinture,
> Bien qu'elle soit d'un pinceau très-vanté,
> Je ne sais quoi d'étrange et d'enchanté
> En l'isolant de l'immense nature,
>
> Ainsi bijoux, meubles, métaux, dorure,
> S'adaptaient juste à sa rare beauté;
> Rien n'offusquait sa parfaite clarté,
> Et tout semblait lui servir de bordure.
>
> Même on eût dit parfois qu'elle croyait
> Que tout voulait l'aimer; elle noyait
> Sa nudité voluptueusement
>
> Dans les baisers du satin et du linge,
> Et, lente ou brusque, à chaque mouvement
> Montrait la grâce enfantine du singe.

The very choice of the sonnet form is, of course, particularly apt for the poet's theme. Its chiseled shape isolates and highlights the mental portrait drawn, setting its images apart—both from "l'immense nature" and from the admiring poet. Presented only indirectly, through third person forms, the beauty of the mistress builds precisely through a series of rhetorical figures. The initial simile comparing the frame of a painting and the "bijoux, meubles, métaux, dorure," that frame the woman's body, the personification of "satin" and "linge" that embrace her, and the closing metaphor that grants the woman the lithe grace of a "singe," all mute her humanity through the power of their referential associations. They produce in the end a strange and enchanting artifact in the reader's mind.

If strategies such as this strongly suggest Baudelaire's participation in the greater Petrarchan tradition, with its almost inevitable sublimation of sex into art, they do not revive the tradition without fundamentally transforming it. The imagery that surrounds, even seems to emanate from, the Baudelairean mistress has acquired a density and opacity not usually associated with poetic portraits of the Renaissance lady. Whether prompting a mental voyage to an exotic paradise lost (as in "Le parfum") or merely highlighting the play of sensorial impressions (as in the visual descriptions of "Les bijoux" and "Un fantome"), Baudelaire's portraits of his mistress charge the reader's mind with a more elaborate, seemingly self-sufficient, imagistic "space." So intense is this metaphoric build that the woman in the Baudelairean love sonnet takes a significantly different role than we have seen in the sonnets of Petrarch and Shakespeare. The Baudelairean mistress neither mirrors the poet's image as Petrarch's transparent plays on "Laura" suggest, nor does she reincarnate it, as do the fair young man and dark mistress of Shakespeare's sonnets. Her effects are far less humanistic. Reified into the third person forms that the poet can only contemplate—cold, hard, and opaque like the "bijoux" she wears—she exemplifies more than a new ideal of beauty. She paints the unbridgeable gulf between the Baudelairean lover and the beloved.

For all its sensuality, Baudelaire's imagery inevitably denotes the poet's estrangement from the woman he describes. As he depicts her in a series of interrelated metaphors, his desire is translated into the power of fantasy, and achieves its consummation in the distanced, referential images of art. Not the poet's mirror so much as his "product," the Baudelairean mistress stands apart, a figment the poet has evidently created but which he can, by definition, never possess. As objective product of the writing self and the very alienation of his desire, Baudelaire's portrait of his mistress thus serves to create another split in the Baudelairean world—a split within the sonnet tradition that fractures as well the lyric self.

Yet even such deft rewritings of conventional sonnet themes and such stirring uses of lyric form gain their full impact only within the collection as a whole. In no way does Baudelaire more dramatically proclaim his awareness of the modern's inner instability and loss of human place than by the larger narrative scheme in which all his sonnets participate. Far from the themes broached by the Renaissance lyric cycles with their almost exclusive concentration on love, Baudelaire aims at a much broader and very different resonance. In the course of the 126 lyrics that produce many individual examples of irony, Baudelaire presents the larger theme or story of a fall, a fall of nature and human nature that the poet evidently sees as the most disconcerting, but most perennial, feature of existence. Whatever narrative line the collection possesses is but the sequential account (through many halting, disjunctive lyric effects) of what for Baudelaire is in fact an intrinsic, irremediable condition. Call it original sin, or the Romantic myth of a paradise lost, what Baudelaire laments is the loss of a world where harmony, divine order, and an integral self can prevail.

If sonnets such as "Correspondances" and "La vie antérieure" sketch something resembling a more harmonious, more auratic world, it is only to better portray its passing. Drawn in a personal key, with continual reference to the poet-writer, and tracing an individual chronology from birth to death, *Les fleurs du mal* paints the world that comes after. The first lyric section, "Spleen et idéal," allows one to gauge the full effects of this fall. Following the poem "Correspondances" and a set of more personalized lyrics, come the three modern love cycles, one addressed to Jeanne Duval, one to Madame Sabatier, and one to Marie Daubrun, each with its distinct but equally unsatisfying renditions of love. Only a few sonnets of escape—notably "La musique" and

"La pipe"—intervene before the onset of the "Spleen" poems that plumb the depths of unhappy humanity. The sonnet entitled "Spleen" epitomizes a central strand of Baudelaire's late nineteenth-century vision:

SPLEEN

Pluviôse, irrité contre la ville entière,
De son urne à grands flots verse un froid ténébreux
Aux pâles habitants du voisin cimetière
Et la mortalité sur les faubourgs brumeux.

Mon chat sur le carreau cherchant une litière
Agite sans repos son corps maigre et galeux;
L'âme d'un vieux poëte erre dans la gouttière
Avec la triste voix d'un fantôme frileux.

Le bourdon se lamente, et la bûche enfumée
Accompagne en fausset la pendule enrhumée,
Cependant qu'en un jeu plein de sales parfums,

Héritage fatal d'une vieille hydropique,
Le beau valet de coeur et la dame de pique
Causent sinistrement de leurs amours défunts.

In typical Baudelairean fashion, the sonnet picture rests upon a series of allegorical personifications: of "Pluviôse," "le bourdon," "la bûche," "la pendule," "le beau valet de coeur," "la dame de pique."

Beginning with a description of the city in the grips of a winter rain falling upon the dead as well as the living, upon the everyday "faubourgs" as well as the uncanny "habitants du voisin cimetière," the poem shortly finds a more internal focus. The personal pronoun "mon" sets the stage for quatrain two and particularly for lines 7 and 8, with their synecdochic glimpse of the poet himself: "L'âme d'un vieux poëte." The sestet then turns to an internal landscape, one in which the most ordinary and most sordid elements of everyday life help convey the spirit of melancholy. Time, as the "bourdon," "bûche," and "pendule" indicate, passes as the stylized, rigidified set of cards speak of now defunct amours. Such

The Baudelairean Sonnet / 121

a depersonalized poem, but one whose psychological import develops an interior landscape, suggests the sinister sense of alienation that is the very essence of spleen.[30] Its disjunctive images project the breakdown of idyllic correspondences into a series of allegorical fragments.

Once produced, such a complete reversal spells no return to the paradisal world evoked earlier in "La vie antérieure" or, even more fully, in "Correspondances." Moments of escape surely exist, but these are for Baudelaire but temporary flights, landing the poet-subject in only greater depths of despair and self-alienation.

The irony so typical of Baudelaire's modern statement flourishes in the three sonnets of "Tableaux parisiens," particularly in the lightninglike flash of hope followed by desolation that has made "A une passante" a classic of urban poetry,[31] and in "Les aveugles," where the portrait of the blind eventually illuminates the spiritual myopia of the poet-subject: "Vois! je me traîne aussi! mais, plus qu'eux hébété, / Je dis: Que cherchent-ils au Ciel, tous ces aveugles?" "Brumes et pluies" ends no more hopefully. If the poem first develops an allegorical correspondence between the poet's interior gloom and the rainy seasons, the closing couplet adds but a final dismal alternative: "par un soir sans lune, deux à deux, / D'endormir la douleur sur un lit hasardeux."

The section entitled "Les fleurs du mal" employs its three sonnets, "La destruction," "Les deux bonnes soeurs" and "La fontaine de sang," to conjure the space of nightmare—of onanism, debauch and death, and hemophilia, respectively. Excluded from the litanies of "Révolte," the sonnet takes a prominent place in the lyric chapters on "Le vin" and "La mort." Especially in the section "La mort," the sonnet helps Baudelaire summon up pictures of promised escape. Death itself, in "La mort des pauvres," supplies "le portique ouvert sur les Cieux inconnus!" Baudelaire even paints the happy ending that death brings the artist. He who in a poem of "Spleen et idéal" feared a poetic sterility sealed by death—"Maint joyau dort enseveli / Dans les ténèbres et l'oubli"[32] —finds this fear effaced by death: "un espoir, étrange et sombre Capitole! / C'est que la Mort, planant comme un soleil nouveau, / Fera s'épanouir les fleurs de leur cerveau!" But in the final sonnet of the collection, "Le rêve d'un curieux," Baudelaire resumes his more usual ironic posture. After awaiting death, in fact after dying, Baudelaire looks beyond, with a surrealistic twist. The final tercet reads:

> J'étais mort sans surprise, et la terrible aurore
> M'enveloppait—Eh quoi! n'est-ce donc que celà?
> La toile était levée et j'attendais encore.

Death brings no change from life and apparently no halt to either self-reflection or despair. The sequence ends in the well-known ode "Le voyage," a poetic account of the speaker's endless search for the new, marked by a no less continual self-speculation.

In the course of these lyric chapters, progressing from the dream of a happier past to the knowledge of continuing despair in death, Baudelaire provides a human perspective in which irony deepens into an abyss, and where the fall of nature and humanity is portrayed as either unredeemed or unalleviated. Whatever comfort this modern vision affords must derive not from what the poet tells us life or death is, but from the artistry—Baudelaire would say from the imagination—by which it is depicted.

POETIC IMAGINATION

Although Baudelaire's determined effort to capture the grim and often evil underside of modernity is one of the distinctive features of his art, his poetry lends itself neither to a simple transcription nor, on the other hand, to a simple transcendence of what he observes. Baudelairean art gathers in the sordidness and despair—but only to engender in the end something more pure, more eternal, more ethically valid. As Baudelaire writes in "Le peintre de la vie moderne": "Il s'agit, pour lui, de dégager de la mode ce qu'elle peut contenir de poétique dans l'historique, de tirer l'éternel du transitoire. . . . La modernité, c'est le transitoire, le fugitif, le contingent, la moitié de l'art, dont l'autre moitié est l'éternel et l'immuable."[33]

For Baudelaire, whatever there is of the eternal arises from what he calls the poetic "imagination," the distinctive temperament that leaves its trace on any work of art that claims importance: "[L'imagination] décompose toute la création, et, avec les matériaux amassés et disposés suivant des règles dont on ne peut trouver l'origine que dans le plus profond de l'âme, elle crée un monde nouveau, elle produit la sensation du neuf."[34] Imagination is the faculty that, the poet asserts, allows him to overcome the all too facile realism he sees around him and to reach toward a more profound expression, a poetry that would gain its power as much from the poet's subjectivity as from the world without: "Qu'est-ce que l'art pur suivant la conception moderne? C'est créer une magie suggestive contenant à la fois l'objet et le sujet, le monde extérieur à l'artiste et l'artiste lui-même."[35]

It is precisely through a poetry that evokes in the reader's mind a strange mingling of subject and object that Baudelaire is able to transform even the most abject theme into something both spiritually uplifting and universal in significance. Through a form well wrought, through a word well chosen, the fallen world that is the modern poet's legacy acquires its beauty and meaning. Language, too, is a thing of the world, a historical entity, but it is something the poet has, to some extent at least, in his own power. It can be polished, renewed. The word, carefully managed, can acquire an almost magical power: "Il y a dans le mot, dans le *verbe*, quelque chose de *sacré* qui nous défend d'en faire un jeu de hasard. Manier savamment une langue, c'est pratiquer une espèce de sorcellerie évocatoire."[36] The sonnet, of course, lends itself particularly well to this insistence on form and language, and it is as much for its inevitable magnification of the poet's craft as for the tradition against which Baudelaire so frequently turns it that the sonnet appears with such frequency in the collection:

> Parce que la forme [du sonnet] est contragnante, l'idée jaillit plus intense: tout va bien au sonnet, la bonhommerie, la galanterie, la passion, la rêverie, la méditation philosophique. Il y a là la beauté du métal ou du minéral travaillés. Avez-vous observé qu'un morceau du ciel aperçu par un soupirail ou entre deux cheminées, deux rochers, ou par une

arcade, donnait une idée plus profonde de l'infini que le grand panorama vu du haut d'une montagne?[37]

As we have begun to see, the sonnet in fact accommodates some of Baudelaire's most terrifying themes and also some of his most serene. And the particular techniques of diction, verse, and figure by which it creates its "sorcellerie évocatoire" are as numerous as its themes. In "Le revenant," for example, Baudelaire manages an eight-syllable line and a series of strong rhyming couplets to create the haunting rhythm of a ghostly passion. Through meter and rhyme alone, a sadistic sentiment acquires its own fascinating beauty and significance. The sonnet "Les aveugles" similarly transfigures the hideous and the tragic—this time primarily through diction and apt use of the sonnet's graphic space. A careful choice of words protects the vision of the physically blind with a certain compassion—"globes ténébreux," "pencher rêveusement leur tête appesantie," "Ils traversent ainsi le noir illimeté, / Ce frère du silence éternel"—as lines move gently, without disturbing interruptions or interjections. To this Baudelaire juxtaposes the clatter of blind city noise—"O cité . . . tu chantes, ris et beugles"—and its damning pleasures, punctuating the whole with a series of halts and exclamations. The very octave-sestet structure underscores this well-worded dichotomy between physical and spiritual blindness.

But nowhere is Baudelaire's ability to manipulate form and language to lend artistic significance to life's passionate attachments and painful transience more acutely felt than in his sonnets on death and love. Though the poet resists the conventional themes and solutions (more likely, as we have seen, is a disintegrating vision such as "Le mort joyeux" or the alienated eroticism of "Les bijoux"), he does at times redeem his painful thematic effects through little more than canny linguistic figurations. It is certainly no accident that the entire section "La mort" contains, except for the long ode "Le voyage," only sonnets, with their power to catch a glimpse of the infinite as if through a "soupirail." It begins with a sonnet that evokes the death of two lovers through a series of artful metonymies and metaphors. While never forgetting the codes of the "real," the poem systematically transfigures them:

LA MORT DES AMANTS

Nous aurons des lits pleins d'odeurs légères,
Des divans profonds comme des tombeaux,
Et d'étranges fleurs sur des étagères,
Ecloses pour nous sous des cieux plus beaux.

Usant à l'envi leurs chaleurs dernières,
Nos deux coeurs seront deux vastes flambeaux,
Qui réfléchiront leurs doubles lumières
Dans nos deux esprits, ces miroirs jumeaux.

Un soir fait de rose et de bleu mystique,
Nous échangerons un éclair unique,
Comme un long sanglot, tout chargé d'adieux;

Et plus tard un Ange, entr'ouvrant les portes,
Viendra ranimer, fidèle et joyeux,
Les miroirs ternis et les flammes mortes.

Baudelaire opens the sonnet by metonymically bonding earthly passion with death. A scene of sensual love with its "lits" and "divans profonds" is charged with pointed references to evanescence and death: "étranges fleurs," "tombeaux." This initial metonymic displacement from a description of the lovers themselves to an evocation of their place gives way in the following quatrain to synecdoche and metaphor. The synecdochic expressions, "nos deux coeurs" and "nos deux esprits," build into traditional metaphors of love: hearts become "deux vastes flambeaux" and souls "ces miroirs jumeaux." On these figural bases, Baudelaire produces the poem's climactic scenes of death (tercet one) and resurrection (tercet two). The image of death appears only through metaphor; the exchange of an "éclair unique" (flashing, presumably, from metaphorical "flambeaux" of the preceding line) is compared to a long "sanglot, tout chargé d'adieux." What follows deepens this metaphoric vein. Though some version of the first person has been present throughout, it disappears in the closing tercet. With an altogether otherworldly omission of person, Baudelaire recalls the lovers through the synecdochic metaphors, "miroirs ternis" and "flammes mortes," to stage a resurrection through the action of an "Ange." And still, though the figuring of death has made art of life's transience, it has not in the process left the earthly behind. The scene of death evokes in its metaphoric torch the ecstasy of a lover's embrace, and in its "long sanglot" the lover's murmur of fulfillment as well as the parting of death. The sonnet's closing metaphors, "miroirs ternis" and "flammes mortes," and the action of the Ange "entr'ouvrant les portes," reopens a question by evoking the poem's first lines. Is the scene to be taken only metaphorically? Is this now the antechamber to paradise? Or is it still but the scene of love with which the sonnet began?

Such a figural tour de force, allowing the poem to hover between the contingency of earthly existence and a sense of eternity, is precisely the sort of craft responsible for the distinctive redemptive "magic" that Baudelaire sought quite consciously to achieve. With such language and such care, *Les fleurs du mal* seems to write its way into the most profound—as well as the most mundane—mysteries of human life and to raise them to rare significance and beauty.

In view of the importance Baudelaire himself attaches to the power of art and the place he gives to the theme of "le poète" in the course of the lyric collection, one would expect him to consistently center and dramatize the lyric persona in individual poems, and to do so through the usual linguistic means. But in fact, the lyric "I" does not occur with the insistence that marks the Petrarchan sonnet or, for that matter, most of the sonnets in the tradition that followed. Though the presence of the Baudelairean persona is equally pervasive, it is far more diffuse than that of either Petrarch or Shakespeare—often linguistically disguised, sometimes perceptible only through a certain use of figure and form. It is a figure that, more often than not, the reader is called upon to write in, detail, and imagine. If in "Le revenant" and "Les aveugles," the "je" makes timely and thematically powerful appearances, in "La mort des amants," for instance, it takes a plural form only to disappear strategically behind a series of metaphoric masks. When we consider this problem further and read "Correspondances," one of Baudelaire's most apparently objective texts, we see that the Baudelairean "je" need not appear at all, even though the whole sonnet rings with an individuality and idiosyncrasy that point to the presence of what Baudelaire would call a distinctive imagination:

CORRESPONDANCES

La Nature est un temple où de vivants piliers
Laissent parfois sortir de confuses paroles;
L'homme y passe à travers des forêts de symboles
Qui l'observent avec des regards familiers.

Comme de longs échos qui de loin se confondent
Dans une ténébreuse et profonde unité,
Vaste comme la nuit et comme la clarté,
Les parfums, les couleurs et les sons se répondent.

Il est des parfums frais comme des chairs d'enfants,
Doux comme les hautbois, verts comme les prairies,
—Et d'autres, corrompus, riches et triomphants,

Ayant l'expansion des choses infinies,
Comme l'ambre, le musc, le benjoin et l'encens,
Qui chantent les transports de l'esprit et des sens.

The sonnet seems in fact an illustration of words written for the "Salon de 1859": "C'est l'imagination qui a enseigné à l'homme le sens moral de la couleur, du contour, du son et du parfum. Elle a créé, au commencement du monde, l'analogie et la métaphore."[38] But how does this "imagination" reveal its particular Baudelairean seal? Certainly the concept of an analogical universe is not Baudelaire's own. A poetics of correspondences, implying "an underlying belief in the unity and connection of all things,"[39] is doubtless an idea as old as humanity. Not only Fourier and Swedenborg, most often cited as probable sources of Baudelaire's poem, but a long poetic and religious tradition had contemplated a world in which all things act as emanations of a divine creator.

Baudelaire's fourteen-line sonnet offers no theoretical additions to these elaborate systems of thought. Still, the poet's subtle emphasis on the human origin of these poetic analogies prevents his sonnet from being a simple restatement. This is all the more remarkable since, in the absence of first and second person pronouns, things rather than persons inevitably predominate. Only their strange juxtapositions seem to summon up the notion of a poetic maker.

Multiple metaphors work to break down the usual linguistic and logical hierarchy by which we categorize the universe as animate and inanimate, as abstract and concrete, as the natural and the civilized, as liquid, solid, and gas. Through the forced joining and realigning of normally segregated ideas, the objective world of nature emerges from the first quatrain as a distinctly human domain. "Nature" is a temple, emitting "paroles." Its symbols lead a life of their own; they can return our glance.

But in this particular sonnet, Baudelaire charges language with even greater human significance. He goes beyond the usual linguistic syntheses offered by similes, metaphors, and identifications to produce an analogy whose references remain highly individualistic. "Correspondances" actually reveals a distinct synesthetic curve, reaching its apex at the sonnet turn. In tercet one, we discover a series of comparisons, all illuminating the olfactory impression of "parfums" through images that are tactile ("chairs d'enfants"), sonoral ("les hautbois"), and visual ("les prairies"). All these "rapports" are established by the explicit interjection of the speaking voice, disclosing its peculiar logic in the reiterating conjunction "comme."

On either side of these explicit correspondences the more implicit synesthesias of metaphor cluster. Quatrain two develops a three-line synesthetic metaphor in the very context of a comparison: the sonoral impression, "de longs échos," appears in a clause whose predicate joins both sound and sight, "se confondent / Dans une ténébreuse et profonde unité." And to conclude the sonnet, Baudelaire builds a synesthetic metaphor whose subject remains olfactory ("parfums"), but whose predicate taps the sonoral ("Qui chantent").

If synesthesia acts, on the one hand, as just another transference, another syntactic combination of the semantically incompatible (another way, that is, by which language establishes a new meaning or a never before apprehended image), it is, on the other hand, the figure most apt to evoke in the reader's mind both the immediacy of human experience and the power of individual art. It reforms the logic we ordinarily attribute to our perceptions, a logic enshrined above all in the social conventions of language. In the process, synesthesia delivers an image of perception that seems, ironically, particularly true to the reader's experience. Human perceptions are notoriously complex. More often than not, they consist of sensorial impressions that are multiple, converging on the single receptive center of what we call the self.[40] Though scarcely confined to a simple translation of immediate perception, and indeed drawing upon the most abstract plane of memory, Baudelaire's use of synesthesia underscores the interpenetration of our bodily senses, allowing perceptual associations to emerge in the form of a particularly complex whole.

Equally important, the synesthetic experience produced in words cannot help but cause the reader to read into the poem a portrait of the human being who writes. Synesthetic figures inevitably conjure up a view of the poet's contact with the external world and his retention of this relationship in memory. Through the power of synesthetic language, associations extend to produce a world that is other, a space without linguistic precedent, one whose ultimate reference can only be the poetic self that the reader imagines.

Thus, in "Correspondances," where the first person function is not explicitly given through any pronoun or first person verb, the succession of figures themselves evokes a novel world of nature, a new universe closely tied to its human focus. A sonnet that begins by transforming "nature" into a "temple" ends by invoking our notions of the human in a much more specific sense. Perfumes issuing from the external world acquire human qualities, celebrate human feelings: Baudelaire exclaims that they "chantent les transports de l'esprit et des sens."

Through the creation of a lyric universe whose logic must be sought in the reader's sense of the poetic mind, Baudelaire draws a vision apparently more private than those of either Petrarch or Shakespeare. It is neither a stylized linguistic order of things, nor an apparently real world of nature that the reader encounters: only a nonrepresentational vision refracted through the prism of a human center. Yet Baudelaire intended his poetry to reach out to more than a restricted elite; indeed, as time has passed, the broad appeal of *Les fleurs du mal* has been proven beyond a doubt. Surely this is due in part to the place Baudelaire found in the lyric for such modern if ungainly themes as city life, human degradation, death, and despair. But it is also due in no small measure to the universality he tapped by prompting his reader to visualize an inward self, by making his poetry quite inevitably a place where external meets internal, where even a description of inanimate objects reflects the complexities of a human observer, where the objective is ultimately indissociable from the most profound reaches of subjectivity.

Tied to poetic craft as he was, Baudelaire was well aware that the language of imagination responds at least in part to indecipherable laws of its own ("des règles dont on ne peut trouver l'origine que dans le plus profond de l'âme").[41] His poetry more than reflects these inner laws. It explores them with full belief in their artistic universality and power. The artists and poets Baudelaire most respected, such as Delacroix and Poe, are those in whom some mysterious fatality seemed to be at work. He goes even so far as to say: "[I]l y a dans les oeuvres issues des profondes individualités quelque chose qui resemble à ces rêves périodiques ou chroniques qui assiégent régulièrement notre sommeil. C'est là ce qui marque le véritable artiste."[42] There is little doubt that Baudelaire found such psychological recesses a fearful region of human reality to plumb, even more so perhaps than the tragic callousness of city life he saw around him. But this too is a part of the human condition, and that which in fact is most universal. Ironically, Baudelaire's exploration of this inner world is, in the end, what makes him most modern. It reveals an intuition into the unconscious that foreshadows Freud. And it leads him to a presentation of self as it had never before appeared in the sonnet tradition: a self not only in process but continually divided, invaded by mysterious and sometimes sinister forces that together produce a terrible fatality, the need to be continually other.

SONNET DREAMS

In many Baudelairean sonnets, language serves to capture a dreamlike sphere of role reversals in which the inanimate and the human blur momentarily within a sonnet frame. Although a line may be drawn between the imaginary mode of dream thought and the more conventional mode of linguistic expression, it is—as Freud later noted—precisely in poetry that these separable modes most freely intermingle. In some of Baudelaire's sonnets of reverie and escape, poetry takes on particularly oneiric qualities.

We have seen that the Baudelairean sonnet quite regularly rejects explicit relationships of cause and effect. Instead, its linear, beginning-to-end movement is converted insofar as possible into a spatial dimension of imagery, while its underlying logical relationships appear as analogy and resemblance, various forms of semantic overlap. The poetic space that this logic creates is filled with vivid, if often quite idiosyncratic, sensorial imagery, while the juxtaposition of images through the beginning-to-end sonnet movement ultimately creates the poem's meaning.

In this, Baudelaire's sonnets differ significantly from those of both Petrarch and Shakespeare. Although a decided preference for more metaphoric structures suggests an apparent kinship with Shakespeare's usual sonnet structure, Shakespeare's choice of the English sonnet form, coupled with his own rhetorical tendencies, produces sonnets with striking oppositions between stanzas. As we have observed, the Baudelairean sonnet tends to do this less, opting for interrelated scenes building a larger sonnet space.

The difference between Shakespeare's and Baudelaire's sonnet structure has, of course, much to do with Baudelaire's more Italianate form whose turn of rhyme at line 9 eliminates the possibly monotonous train of three successive quatrains. One might have thought that the Continental heritage of the Baudelairean form would tie his sonnet structures more closely to some of those particularly metaphoric sonnets showing up from time to time in the *Rime sparse* and in the works of Petrarch's Italian, English, and French followers. But Baudelaire's rhetorical penchant makes his analogical sonnets altogether unique. While Petrarch's sonnets, whether analogical or "progressive," often contain a logical node at the sonnet's center that separates an initial image from the conclusion, such explicit transtextual logic rarely governs Baudelaire's texts. Instead, sonnet after sonnet binds images together through semantic overlaps of a less evident nature—through joint reliance upon a single metaphor or simply through the re-presentation of a single image, originally taking shape in a title or opening quatrain and then modified from stanza to stanza or sentence to sentence. Usually Baudelaire's sonnet draws its rapports by more implicit means. Such rapports are far more often to be inferred by the reader than declared by a reasoning voice.

These features characterize some of the sonnets we have already examined in detail. "La vie antérieure" draws a single canvas, marked above all by a subtle change in focus. A title and opening imagery provide the unity for sonnets such as "Correspondances," "Le flambeau vivant," and "Spleen." "La musique" proceeds by pressing a single metaphor from the sonnet's beginning to its end, and succeeds in temporarily drawing music and self into a single imaginative space, whereas "La mort des amants" creates its scenes of death and resurrection by carefully modulating a single set of figures.

Baudelaire's disregard for causal logic is doubtless deliberate. It is yet another, and very effective, way to deny any sense of realism or naturalism. By defying traditional marks of chronology and rationalization, Baudelaire's sonnets tend all the more to the "surnaturel." At the same time, this avoidance brings them closer to a more unconscious, even oneiric logic, a logic perhaps more universal in its reach.

The syntax of dream, as Freud describes it, reveals the same logical principles on which the Baudelairean sonnet so often rests. It too is distinguished by a disregard for causal and temporal relationships: "One and only one of these logical relations is very highly favored by the mechanism of dream formation: namely, the relationship of similarity, consonance, or approximation, the relationship of 'just as.'"[43] Through such syntactic patterns, the temporal flow of dream time, like the linguistic time of the Baudelairean sonnet, is transposed into the spatial, the imagistic.

The Baudelairean sonnet evokes the dream in another way too, in its dependence upon sensorial imagery, an imagery primarily visual but often invoking other senses as well.[44] There is, of course, a major difference between dream and poem. If the imaginary world of dream derives its pictures from the abyss of intellectually disorganized sense impressions housed in the unconscious, the poet, confined to ordinary language, necessarily draws upon mental pictures already socialized and thus conventionalized. The linguistic sign has already accomplished a parceling out of reality, and the poet's effects inevitably depend upon his choice and manipulation of these conventional signs.

When Baudelaire's lexical choices are examined in the abstract of a concordance, they are, if anything, less revolutionary than one might expect. A substantial number of words recur with some frequency in *Les fleurs du mal*, revealing particular perceptions of reality, as well as distinctly Baudelairean obsessions: "nuit," "corps," "soir," "fond," "mer," "sang," "bras," "enfant," "baisers," "pleurs," "ténèbres," "poète," "horreur," "gouffre," "enfer."[45] Though we may regard this group of frequently appearing terms as unmistakable signs of the poet's preoccupations, it constitutes but part of Baudelaire's lexical practice. Among his most often used terms, we also find the quite traditional lyric array of "coeur," "yeux," "âme," "amour," as well as words providing the classical segmentation of reality into "ciel," "air," "terre," and "feu."[46]

Still, Baudelaire's use of these less vivid terms is much more measured than Petrarch's. Unlike the Petrarchan text, the Baudelairean seldom allows an abstract, relatively nondenotative sign to stand alone, or to lose any small image-making power it may possess in the temporal progression of the sonnet's meaning. Instead, these more general terms tend to receive pictorial reinforcement from more precise qualifiers or predicates. Together, the words form their often vivid scenes.

Equally important, the Baudelairean sonnet's novel rhetorical strategies, with their usual culmination in some combined form of irony and allegory, make different use of the third person nouns that, in both Petrarch's and Shakespeare's sonnets, always remain fully personalized, enveloped in the dominant figures of self and/or related to a beloved other. Baudelaire's sonnet visions derive their relatively vast expanse of sonnet space precisely from the fact that third person nouns are dominated by neither the first person (as regularly happens in the Petrarchan text) nor by the linguistic encounter of two human beings (as in the Shakespearean). In the Baudelairean sonnet, referential things may stand alone, may remain grammatically and semantically subject. Less constricted by a world of persons, an external world of things may expand freely in the space of the reader's mind.

In "La pipe," for instance, a sonnet particularly appreciated by Proust, Baudelaire's inanimate images demonstrate their supernatural power:

LA PIPE

Je suis la pipe d'un auteur;
On voit, à contempler ma mine
D'Abyssinienne ou de Cafrine,
Que mon maître est un grand fumeur.

Quand il est comblé de douleur,
Je fume comme la chaumine
Où se prépare la cuisine
Pour le retour du laboureur.

J'enlace et je berce son âme
Dans le réseau mobile et bleu
Qui monte de ma bouche en feu,

> Et je roule un puissant dictame
> Qui charme son coeur et guérit
> De ses fatigues son esprit.

The sonnet's fourteen lines show an exemplary combination of more ordinary, nondenotative words and unusual, extremely precise and denotative ones. Thus, such semantically flat terms as "mine," "feu," and "coeur," when they do occur, do not stand alone. In each case, they are bound to more precise, denotative words so that together they conjure a series of vivid images. Qualifying "mine," for instance, with "d'Abyssinienne ou de Cafrine" leads us out of the ordinary toward an exotic and, in any case, more concrete picture of the speaking "pipe." "En feu," on the other hand, appears in line 11 as the qualification of "bouche." Together they conjure a unique personification. Likewise, "coeur" acts within a phrase modifying the far more unusual expression "puissant dictame."

Such imagery actually sets the stage for an internal drama, and the quite extraordinary role of the "je" within the text only reinforces the sonnet's oneiric qualities. In "La pipe," Baudelaire suggests a peculiarly dreamlike pattern far removed from the play of self that we have seen in the Petrarchan and Shakespearean sonnets. The sonnet becomes the unlimited province of the "moi," a place where the subject appears in its most veiled and perplexing forms, but also where it can reveal its most naked meanings.

As in the dream as Freud presents it, the "moi" is here implicit in everything described.[47] Images are not simply pictures, that is, but intense re-presentations and objectifications of aspects, situations, and desires of the self. It is an imagery from which the self is not only never absent, but in which it appears in all of its psychic complexity. It appears in process, never integral, but split, ironic to its very core.

Lexically based thematic analyses of *Les fleurs du mal* succeed in discovering a recurring pattern of words and images. P. Guiraud, for instance, finds Baudelaire's universe to look something like this:[48]

                    L'azur

La Mer   Ici   Le Vin
Là-bas   Paradis artificiels
                    Le gouffre

It is, curiously, a poetic cosmology from which the self is conspicuously absent. Or rather, it is not a world that revolves about a central directing self, but one in which the self figures only as an assumed part of all that is more objective, referential, external. The poet-persona relates to the different spheres of his poetic world, to be sure. But he does so metaphorically rather than metonymically. His appearance within the text is generally based upon various, often tenuous identifications of the self with the images formed.

The sonnets analyzed here illustrate several ways by which a third person world may represent the speaker. The self may be interpolated into the imagistic or cognitive sphere through relatively self-referential figures such as comparison and synesthesia. In sonnets such as "Correspondances," then, the third person imagery seems to emanate from a subjective presence rather than exist alone, objective and totally separable from the poet-writer. Although the poetic dialogue, such as we saw at work in Shakespeare's sonnet, may well occur in Baudelaire's poems, it is just as often a dialogue addressed to the external world as to a person.[49] In these ways, external things are humanized, while simultaneously identified with the writing self.

Even when the self appears more directly, the "moi" is frequently doubled, disguised, split, alienated by synecdoche, or masked by a third person label such as "l'auteur" or "le poëte." At times, when the speaking self, the "je," comes to the fore most clearly and most dramatically, more than one being may in fact coexist and thereby complicate the role of the first person voice.[50] Such overdetermination creates the dreamlike richness of "La pipe." Here, where the poetic self is already doubled in the third person form "l'auteur," the "je" takes on a third person role in the impersonation of the pipe. This reversal of persons—where the first person form is applied to a thing normally expressed through the third, and a third person form carries the semantic weight of the poetic self—provides a verbal dramatization of the confusions and transformations of self and other that so often occur in the purely imaginary space of dream or in the "paradis artificiel" of hashish, where the censorship of the conscious mind is reduced before the play of the unconscious.[51] In this sonnet of escape, the fact that "je est un autre" is far less alienating than one might expect. The theme of enclosure develops at the sonnet turn, as if to counteract the undeniable distancing of the poetic self.

Each stanza of "La pipe" presents a complete poetic picture. And, in typical Baudelairean fashion, the movement from sonnet beginning to end unites the juxtaposed images in a portrait of the pipe and its relationship to the author. The first quatrain describes the pipe externally as well as in relationship to the disguised "moi": "On voit . . . Que mon maître est un grand fumeur." From this initial portrait flow three other image groups, each specifying the pipe's reaction to the master's "douleur." Thought thus develops neither causally nor temporally, but only through thematic resemblances: each scene interprets somewhat differently the comfort being offered the "auteur."

The most vivid of the sonnet's three closing images is doubtless that of tercet one, where two instances of "je" personify the pipe and create the central image of encircling, lulling fumes: "J'enlace et je berce son âme / Dans le réseau mobile et bleu / Qui monte de ma bouche en feu." In this surreal sphere, where a third person thing speaks a fourteen-line monologue, the world of the "other" becomes one with the desires of the self. The imagery that follows implies even more clearly why the poet is a "grand fumeur." His pipe, like the sonnet which bears its name, provides the access to dream, a place of "bercement," where the real disappears into a brief imaginary oblivion. The sonnet, again like a dream, projects a wish fulfilled, here an exotic lullaby.

Though "La pipe" offers a perhaps exaggerated example of Baudelaire's capacity to produce an oneiric world of the self, it is in some ways quite typical of the sonnets of *Les fleurs du mal* and, what is more, is particularly helpful in delineating Baudelaire's relationship to the long sonnet tradition in which he so prominently figures. For sonnets such as this reveal the underlying reason why allegory and irony are so unusually difficult to distinguish in Baudelaire's poetics and why he himself used a loose and changing terminology to describe his rhetorical techniques. The sensation of space that Baudelaire regularly conjures through his sonnet rhetoric is, regardless of its apparent theme and dominant rhetorical structure, always the space of the self, its existence in a modern and frequently alienating world. Georges Poulet states it this way: "En se rendant sensible l'espace, la pensée de Baudelaire se rend visible le temps, c'est à dire se rend visible l'étendue de l'existence."[52]

Produced as much from an inward as from an outward gaze, Baudelaire's poetry projects an awareness that the self is a nondelimitable sphere, one in which internal and external intermingle. To put it another way, the Baudelairean lyric self becomes, even in the restricted space of the sonnet form, a forever disintegrating, fissured being. As the artist had been displaced in his social function until he was just one of many human hands laboring in a busy urban society, so his view of self and world mark out a terrible contingency. It is a self that can only be defined, so it seems, in its often haphazard relationship to all that is other, to thing as well as person. And rather than strive to present itself as a powerful, controlling entity, it is a self that is always in the process of a seemingly helpless, sometimes mystic duplication and multiplication—and always intent on describing this. Baudelaire declares this more than once in his journals:

> Le plaisir d'être dans les foules est une expression mystérieuse de la jouissance de la multiplication du nombre. . . . *Tout* est nombre. Le nombre est dans *tout*. Le nombre est dans l'individu. L'ivresse est un nombre.[53]
>
> Ivresse religieuse des grandes villes.—Panthéisme. Moi, c'est tous; tout, c'est moi.
> Tourbillon.[54]

The sonnets themselves frequently bear witness to this attempt to highlight a multiplication—and division—of self into world, world into self. Thus, we may find that the sonnet's central turn, produced by the French octave-sestet form, serves a different function than what we have seen in the sonnet practice of Petrarch and Shakespeare. Here it often acts precisely as the place where an allegorical identity of self and world is most pronounced, an identity generally maintained as the sonnet proceeds toward closure and, at times, an ironic fall. In "Le flambeau vivant," for instance, where the lyric self appears explicitly in first person possessive and object pronouns, a first person subject pronoun nonetheless awaits line 7 to make its dramatic entrance. And it is here that the relationship between self and "les yeux" is most clearly posed: "Ils sont mes serviteurs et je suis leur esclave; / Tout mon être obéit à ce vivant flambeau." "La musique" likewise contains the greatest concentration of first person forms about the sonnet turn, particularly in line 9's "Je sens vibrer en moi toutes les passions / D'un vaisseau qui souffre," where self and image of the sea are most closely bound. In "La vie antérieure," the self enters through two first person subject pronouns and, with the second, appearing at the sonnet turn, takes a place at the very center of the paradisal world. "Correspondances," in which no pronouns refer to the self, allows figures alone to trace a self-referential meaning through the particularly explicit synesthesias of quatrain two. And in "Spleen," the poet, alienated and disguised in a third person synecdoche—"l'âme d'un vieux poëte erre dans la gouttière"—takes a role only in line 7, in the midst of the sinister inner scene created.

In his structural centering of a split and mobile self, Baudelaire again rejoins, while setting his remarkable seal of difference upon, a long sonnet tradition. Like Petrarch and Shakespeare, who used the sonnet's turn to engage the reader in the contemplation of powerful, if continually questioning and sometimes reincarnated selves, Baudelaire used the same turn to engage the reader in the contemplation of a self literally always in the process of definition, through its inward gaze and its outward-looking analogies. Yet, to be sure, a deconstruction of self—and with it of a stable and centered world—had always been a fact of language and therefore a part of being human. Baudelaire's task, and a historically inevitable one at that, was not at all his discovery of the self's inevitable division and historical contingency, but rather his desire to make this theme as overt, as vivid, as possible. And in this, Baudelaire brings to the sonnet a new sense of its textuality, its inability to close its significance, its tendency to leave itself anaphorically open. His keen awareness of and willingness to explore the power of language in relation to what he saw as the hidden laws of individual genius brought with it a sonnet that questioned the very rules of its form as it revised its most important themes.

If Eliot would be among the first major poets to take up Baudelaire's fascination with the modern city, Verlaine, Mallarmé and, later, Valéry would likewise look to Baudelaire as a master of the modern lyric, of the modern self, and also of the modern sonnet. It would in fact be among those of Baudelaire's successors who called themselves surrealists and symbolists that the sonnet would reach a new height of popularity in France. And at least in part through the practice of its form, the modernism Baudelaire himself initiated would begin a process of modification and transformation that would continue from the late nineteenth century to our own day.

Conclusion

This study began by acknowledging the mysterious quality of the sonnet. A mystery that touches the semantic range the form permits, it extends as well to the sonnet's complex relationship to literary tradition and, most particularly, to the form's unusual longevity. The mystery only intensifies as we read individual sonnets by individual poets. Resisting a simple reliance upon the sonnet's repetitive qualities of form and tradition, the most interesting sonnets seem to lead the reader centrifugally, from a sense of the form's more or less invariable qualities to the illumination of dramatic differences in rhetoric and meaning.

As we have seen, Petrarch, Shakespeare, and Baudelaire each chose the traditional fourteen-line sonnet with turns either at line 8 (in the Italian and French) or at line 12 (in the Shakespearean), and thus remained well within the established formal bounds of the genre. But each poet used language to open up new and exciting worlds of thought and emotion. Petrarch, with his love for the classical past and keen sense of individual style, polished a rhetoric that powerfully foregrounded the artistic maker. His "visible grammar" emphasizes the performance of a speaking self within a dramatically articulated syntax—modulated by pauses, inversions, and postponements of meaning. Supporting this central performance is his highly defined, well-regulated, and frequently repeated system of images, all building the figure of a poet-persona and his unending desire. Petrarch's metonymic grammar, articulating his themes of displacement and desire, generally emphasizes the sonnet's potential for a linear, sequential development of thought. This temporal emphasis, often underscored by phonic effects of assonance and alliteration, only intensifies the strong semantic transformation that generally occurs around line 8, precisely where the performing "io" tends to assert itself most.

Through these combined techniques, Petrarch displays his classical penchant and his newfound sense of a rhetorical voice, freed from allegorical restraint. He also establishes a major European lyric style, his own rhetorical voice becoming the standard against which subsequent poets will measure their own. Indeed, after Petrarch, the sonnet begins to carry far more psychological weight than it had when Giacomo da Lentino or Dante used it. For centuries, in fact, a strong if questioning lyric "I" dominated the genre's subthemes of love, nature, spiritual angst, and death, prompting readers to imagine the psyche to which the "I" referred. It took a well-articulated sense of language and self to open this tradition to new possibilities. Sidney's *Astrophil and Stella* went far to accomplish this, as did Spenser's *Amoretti*, Milton's sonnets and, above all, the collection we know as Shakespeare's *Sonnets*.

Shakespeare, whose *Sonnets* bring the Renaissance sonnet vogue to climactic completion, in fact reworked some of Petrarch's most salient themes—but from a fresh, highly individual viewpoint. Instead of emphasizing a complex syntax, grammatical involution, and the constant yearning for a displaced and ultimately mirroring lady, Shakespeare builds an invisible syntax of imagery, displaying its power through rapidly changing metaphors that can be seen only in the associative dimensions of the reader's mind. Rather than draw attention to the play of words and the voice that speaks them, Shakespeare's syntax works toward a vertical reach of language that inspires the reader to imagine a separate, full-bodied world.

Yet Shakespeare's more metaphoric emphasis, with its stirring re-presentations of life's beauty and pain, plays out its full significance only in the compelling drama he stages between "I" and "thou." For in Shakespeare's *Sonnets*, the lyric persona does not simply assert its considerable poetic power. It reveals a newfound confidence as it reincarnates aspects of itself in two other human figures, the "fair young man" and the "dark lady." Imagery helps build these three distinct "persons" and a sense of dramatic encounter new to the sonnet tradition. Precisely this "I"-"thou" configuration helps contain Shakespeare's often complex play of metaphor, pun, and paradox. Though pressing at times to the very limits of representation, Shakespeare's witty style finds its ultimate mimetic purpose in depicting this distinctly human world. And so, within each Shakespeare sonnet, with its more loosely structured form, a miniature drama unfolds. Its rapid alternations of analogy and opposition come to a close with a first or second person utterance that lends a reassuringly human dénouement to the unsettling complications that precede it.

Though Shakespeare's *Sonnets* could hardly have been more tied to the tradition it deftly revised, the sequence virtually ended the sonnet's Renaissance phase. Unlike Petrarch's *Rime sparse* and for historical reasons that surpass Shakespeare's own practice, his *Sonnets* could not impose on the English or European sonnet an influential period style. Rather, his revolutionary use of the sonnet found its most immediate echoes in larger lyric forms, as well as in the drama and narrative, which his well-defined sonnet personae and their "plot" prefigure. But with the rise of these more capacious forms, the sonnet itself was gradually abandoned until, in the eighteenth century, it all but disappeared.

When the sonnet finally regains popularity in the nineteenth century, it brings with it a new interest in poetry's graphic, spatial dimensions. The sonnets of Baudelaire's *Les fleurs du mal*, our third example of difference-within-repetition, offer just such spatial, image-conscious structures, built through a style tempted less by metonymy or metaphor than by the joint potential of irony and allegory.

Through a rhetoric that seems to halt the temporal movement of language, Baudelaire paints poetic canvasses that effectively project time into the space of imagery. Employing neither the grammatical involutions of Petrarch, nor the metamorphoses of imagery so typical of Shakespeare, Baudelaire imposes on the sonnet an altogether novel face. It is one which, more like Petrarch than Shakespeare, points to its own artistry. But it does so not by a metonymic style or an emphasis upon a strong performing self, but by a deft use of allegory and irony that touches the lyric "I" as well. Underscoring the specifically linguistic character of poetry and its distance from direct re-presentation, Baudelaire's irony and allegory eventually highlight only a split, schismatic image of the poetic self. At times, the self seems virtually to disappear (at least as a visible "I"), though such an absence usually ends merely by urging the reader to imagine more powerfully this elusive persona. Here, the sonnet's long history doubtless plays a role, for it reinforces our expectations that at the very heart of the sonnet, a self will somehow assert its importance. Baudelaire's writing, with its pervasive confusion of subject and object, its anaphoric discourse pointing more to other words than to clear and distinct ideas of world and self, paves the way to a new era of writing. It reminds us that the notion of a strong, governing subject, a transcendental "I," is a historically shaped phenomenon—one no more natural or inevitable than Baudelaire's split and elusive persona.

From this summary, we can conclude that the works of Petrarch, Shakespeare, and Baudelaire abundantly illustrate rhetorical difference, even revolutionary change. Actually, we can say more than this. As I have tried to show in the preceding chapters, the distinctive rhetoric of these three poets in fact reveals some of the best known, most diverse types of lyric poetry. Their differences—which challenge the hegemony of metaphor and symbol to include metonymy, irony, and allegory—also fit quite neatly another, better-known set of poetic categories. Ezra Pound, thinking back no doubt to Coleridge's poetry of the eye, the word, and the ear, divided all poetry into three distinct types.[1] Each strongly shapes the sonnets of one of the three poets we have considered. *Melopoeia*, or "music-making," echoes in Petrarch's temporal, metonymic emphasis with its plays on sound and meaning. *Logopoeia*, or "word-making," governs Shakespeare's witty wordplay, his puns and paradoxes, and *phanopoeia*, or "image-making," is perfectly visible in Baudelaire's sometimes ironic, sometimes allegorical portraits of the human condition.

Moreover, though Pound unfortunately does not account for

the lyric self in his famous triad, the three sorts of self-presentation most commonly associated with lyric poetry also help mould these lyric collections.[2] In Petrarch's *Rime sparse*, we find the prototypical "meditative poem," to borrow Eliot's phrase. Here the poet talks to himself or to no one in particular. If there is an addressee, it is abstract or inanimate, a thing which (like the metonymic displacements and synecdochic fragmentations of Laura) does little more than focus the subjective meditations of the speaker. Shakespeare's *Sonnets*, with their more dramatic emphasis, exemplify the "I"-"thou" form in which the poet addresses or pretends to address another person. With Shakespeare, this addressee becomes a metaphoric "other" of the speaking self, as well as a mediating figure for the reader. Most often, this "I"-"thou" form arises in intensely dramatic situations in which the personal relationship, its particular story, reveals itself in the speaker's praise or blame. Finally, in the sonnets of Baudelaire (which do sometimes participate in the "I"-"thou" pattern), the "I" more often sets the standard for modernist verse. It disappears from the page entirely, presenting its vision without pronominal intervention, acting rather as medium for the imagery the sonnets display.

Semantic range, then, the sonnet has. And this capacity alone provides one clue to its longevity. Flexibility doubtless ranks high on any poet's list of formal prerequisites. Still, this flexibility can hardly take sole responsibility for the sonnet's mysterious longevity. For why, we must ask, was the sonnet so attractive from the first and why, at certain, well-defined points in literary history, has it exerted an almost irresistible appeal? Although one can never claim certainty in such matters, some explanatory value might be found in this: From its beginnings, the sonnet has emphasized, regardless of individual style and theme, precisely those characteristics most frequently associated with post-Renaissance lyric as a whole—a musical construction and a high degree of subjectivity, a concentration on the "I."[3] In short, the sonnet is particularly, even archetypically, lyrical.

The musical quality of lyric is, of course, the quality longest associated with it. Classical poetics defines the lyric as poetry that is sung or chanted, accompanied by musical instruments. With the Renaissance, this sort of description no longer strictly applied. Nonetheless, poetry called lyric did retain a certain representation of music through its sound patterns, its versification. The sonnet's careful repetition of meter and rhyme (from its birth, we recall, it does not seem to have required musical accompaniment) inevitably confers upon it precisely such musical qualities, as well as a distinctive, asymmetrical unity. Very likely, it was this unusual sophistication in a brief and manageable form that first drew poets to it and encouraged a private, meditative attitude. Even today, when writers so often alter its rhyme scheme, the mere presence of a symmetrical two-part structure for fourteen lines preserves enough of its form to allow its distinctive musical architecture to emerge.

Historically, the lyric has also made the speaking "I" its imaginative focus. From Plato's discussion of the three types of narration in the *Republic*, to Coleridge in the *Biographia Literaria*, to structuralist discussions of the lyric "I,"[4] the lyric mode has been described at least partly through its representation of a speaking self. Since the Romantic period, such subjectivity has often become the lyric's defining quality.

This concentration on a poetic self certainly marks the sonnets of Petrarch, Shakespeare, and Baudelaire. Whether striving for prominence and centrality or ruminating upon its constant fissures, the lyric "I" in fact remains the focal point of all three collections. In this respect, each poet's work exemplifies Paul Fussell's judgment on the sonnet in general, as depicting a "highly personal . . . attitude toward experience."[5] But then, it is perhaps even the case (though this thought must remain purely conjectural) that one reason the lyric self so easily dominates the sonnet is that the musical construction of the form encourages this. At the place in the sonnet where one thought modulates to another, where imagery powerfully metamorphoses—here, at the sonnet turn, the lyric "I" tends to appear in its most characteristic light. Though a particularly forceful subjectivity does not inevitably occur at this point, it does return with striking regularity. And perhaps this is not so very surprising. At the sonnet turn the poet must strive hardest to transform meaning in an interesting and, if possible, an exciting way. No wonder he or she often leaves here the human imprint of a persona.

Perhaps for reasons such as these, the sonnet has remained an important genre for some 600 years, waxing and waning in popularity with the changing fortunes of the greater lyric tradition. Admittedly, this statement deserves some qualification. For the sonnet has, we recall, flourished most in two distinct periods: first in the Renaissance and then in the late Romantic, early modernist era—both of them moments when self, language, and lyric form underwent major changes. The sonnet, with its compact musical construction and subjective focus, was well adapted to help foster these changes.

In the Renaissance, the sonnet certainly took a particularly active role, for its short, elegant form helped poets advance their careful polishing of the European vernaculars. If it was largely due to Petrarch's *Rime sparse* that the Italian vernacular was first accepted as a "noble" tongue, the vogue of sonnet writing he began encouraged other poets to perfect their own national languages. Even England, whose Renaissance tradition decidedly continued its medieval past, found in the sonnet an excellent literary apprenticeship. In fact, almost every major Renaissance poet in Italy, France, and England (as well as in Spain and Germany) used the form, a challenge in its own right, and fine preparation for longer, more complex works the poet might attempt. Here the poet could try a difficult verse pattern and, by repeating a series of traditional themes, reveal an individual variation in style. Indeed, the perfection of the vernacular in light of classical ideals inevitably produced more than rhetorical eloquence. It also gave birth to an exciting, humanistic quest for a distinctive persona.

The Renaissance once past, the sonnet's popularity quickly waned. When it returned to favor later, in Romantic and post-Romantic poetry, it came to ease another transition. At a point when the literary text no longer needed to build the power of language and self (it had, by then, been amply demonstrated), the sonnet began to convey a very painful awareness of linguistic and human contingency. Looking back to the Renaissance and to an active Romantic revival of the lyric, Baudelaire—and later, Mallarmé—injected the sonnet with a highly antimimetic, antisymbolic style, whose themes extended well beyond traditional meditations on nature and love, and often depended upon a supple flexing of the sonnet's rigid verse patterns. Through the work of such poets, the sonnet's focused form breaks into the abyss that is the human psyche and explores the impossible desire of language to repeat, to re-present an external world. Perhaps these poets found in the sonnet a manageable space in which to create their nonrepresentational artistic world. Perhaps too their concern with language, self, and poetic form found in the sonnet an important point of reference within a changing tradition. A mere repetition of its musical patterns helped ground the revolutionary poetics of the modernist era, while simultaneously favoring the new, often more spatially conscious aspirations of its poets.

Baudelaire, of course, stands only at the threshold of this modern literary period. Since his time, versification itself has suffered enormous change, relaxing more rigid structures to make room for new, free verse patterns. In the recognized crisis of lyric form and meaning that has characterized a significant strain of poetry written between the late nineteenth century and our own day, the sonnet, with its clear ties to the past and its evocation of a poetic self, has taken a paradoxical position. It is a form as much to be worked against, even overcome, as it is to be recalled and cultivated.

As such, the sonnet has attracted a surprising number of the most important voices in modern poetry: Rainer Maria Rilke, George Meredith, Gerard Manley Hopkins, Stéphane Mallarmé, W. H. Auden, and Wallace Stevens, to name but a few. Through revisions of its length and rhyme scheme, the sonnet has often tried to keep pace with the challenge to lyric form brought by trends in contemporary poetry. For instance, if Meredith's "Modern Love" is a sequence of sixteen-line poems, Stevens's "Le monocle de mon oncle" merely suggests the sonnet sequence through a series of eleven-line unrhymed poems. Hopkins experimented with the "curtal" or curtailed sonnet and Auden with expanded forms, while varieties in rhyme scheme particularly appealed to Mallarmé. Still, the modern sonnet has remained for all this a recognizable form, and one that carries with it strong echoes of the past. The sheer particularity, the recognizability of the sonnet's musical construction, inevitably endows it with historical resonance, and its most effective writers have not failed to exploit this. From this point of view, centuries of repetition have served only to hone the sonnet form, making it a more perfect instrument for defining a thematic and formal stance, for advancing it dramatically as an individual instance in a growing community of texts.

A particularly good example of the historically self-conscious modern sonnet is the collection by John Berryman, called, simply, *Berryman's Sonnets*. Looking directly to Petrarch and the Renaissance tradition, these poems carefully strike their unmistakable difference. In a sonnet such as "Swarthy when young; who took the tonsure; sign," Berryman underscores his own poetic narrative and its distance from Petrarch's, as much through rhetoric as through theme. But in good Petrarchan fashion, his voice speaks most strongly at the traditional turn between octave and sestet. Here he specifically measures his own, new voice against its lyric precursor:

> Swarthy when young; who took the tonsure; sign,
> His coronation, wangled, his name re-said
> For euphony; off to courts fluttered, and fled;
> Professorships refused; upon one line
> Worked years; and then that genial concubine.
> Seventy springs he read, and wrote, and read.
> On the day of the year his people found him dead
> I read his story. Anew I studied mine.
>
> Also there was Laura and three-seventeen
> Sonnets to something like her . . . twenty one years.
> He never touched her. Swirl our crimes and
> crimes.
> Gold-haired (too), dark-eyed, ignorant of rimes
> Was she? Virtuous? The old brume seldom clears.
> —Two guilty and crepe-yellow mouths
>   Lise! be our bright surviving actual scene.[6]

For modern sonnets such as this, Dante Gabriel Rosetti's definition seems hardly out of date: "A sonnet is a moment's monument— / Memorial from the soul's eternity / to one deathless hour."[7] It preserves the moment, but only through the reach to a now almost mythic past, an "eternity" of soul—but also of voices that resonate in the single utterance.

The sonnet's remarkable power to summon a tradition in which the human self has been central, if questioned, and in which the very repetition of form brings to mind a heady swim of differences, fortifies its appeal to the writer and the reader of today. But, we may still ask, will the sonnet continue to survive? Current interest in it by poets as different as Seamus Heaney, Adrienne Rich, Philippe Jaccottet, André Frénaud, and Allen Ginsberg suggests that, for the foreseeable future, the answer is yes. In fact, I think it probable that as long as a musical structure and the image of a lyric self continue to interest the poet, the sonnet will be called on now and then to highlight these signs of human artistry and power. And by invoking a venerable past through its form, it will enable the contemporary poet to speak in whatever style individual talent allows—but always with a long and powerful lyric history to set his or her words into relief.

Notes

INTRODUCTION

1. Oppenheimer, "The Origin of the Sonnet," p. 302.
2. See Coleridge, *The Statesman's Manual, Collected Works*, Vol. VI, p. 30, for the distinction between allegory and symbol. Wayne Booth comments on the current scholarly fascination with metaphor in "Metaphor as Rhetoric," p. 47. See also Genette, "La rhétorique restreinte," *Figures III*, pp. 21–40.
3. For a discussion of the sonnet's history from an international perspective, see Mönch, *Das Sonett*.

CHAPTER ONE

1. Petrarca, *Canzoniere*, ed. Contini, p. 49. I have quoted from this edition throughout.
2. See especially Liber Tertius, *Secretum*, in Petrarca, *Prose*, pp. 131–215.
3. Contini, "Preliminari sulla lingua del Petrarca," *Varianti*, p. 179.
4. See Vellutello, *Il Petrarca*, for an early example of an autobiographical criticism. The tradition continues in the poetic rubrics of Giacomo Leopardi's commentary, *Rime di Francesco Petrarca*.
5. Wilkins, *The Invention of the Sonnet*, pp. 11–39.
6. Sapegno, *Disegno storico*, p. 15.
7. Oppenheimer, "The Origin of the Sonnet," pp. 294–95.
8. For excellent discussions and a bibliography of the complex topic of courtly love, see Ferrante and Economou, *In Pursuit of Perfection*. I am using the term *courtly love* here to refer to what these authors call its "essential assumptions": namely, "the nobility of the lover, the sometimes inseparable distance between him and the lady, the exalting nature of his

devotion, and the social context of the love," p. 5. There is little doubt that themes associated with courtly love survived into European Renaissance literature and that they were particularly spurred on by Petrarch's poetry. What is equally fascinating and will be considered in chapters to follow is the persistence of such themes in sonnets of the nineteenth and twentieth centuries.

9. Alighieri, *De vulgari eloquentia*, pp. 184–86. Dante states specifically that he leaves his treatment of the ballata and the sonnet to the fourth book of the treatise, where the "volgare mezzano" will be discussed. Unfortunately, Dante finished only two of the four books intended. Cf. Oppenheimer, "The Origin of the Sonnet," pp. 295–97, for a discussion of Dante's theory of the sonnet.

10. Petrarca, Introduction to *Petrarch's Lyric Poems*, translated and edited by Durling, pp. 10–11.

11. Sonnino, *A Handbook*, p. 244; Lanham, *A Handlist*, pp. 101–3.

12. See, for instance, line 1 of "Solo e pensoso," where hyperbaton juxtaposes subject and object in an opening statement. Through a grammatical figure, Petrarch captures the close relationship between poet and nature that develops throughout the poem. Clearly, this is a case where the order and arrangement of words directly affect meaning, even if less forcefully than a trope might allow.

13. See Berni's "Capitolo a Fra Bastiano del Piombo," *Opere burlesche*, pp. 27–29.

14. See Jakobson and Halle, *Fundamentals of Language*, esp. "The Twofold Character of Language," pp. 58–62 and "The Metaphoric and Metonymic Poles," pp. 76–82.

15. References to "cognitive" and "performative"—as related to "metaphoric" and "metonymic"—derive largely from De Man, *Allegories of Reading*, esp. pp. ix, 3–19, 59–67. Their purpose and meaning are, however, somewhat different here.

16. Jakobson and Hall, *Fundamentals of Language*, p. 81.

17. See Le Guern, *Sémantique*, esp. pp. 23–28. See also Jakobson and Hall, *Fundamentals of Language*, pp. 58–62, 76–82.

18. Jakobson and Halle, *Fundamentals of Language*, p. 81. On desire as metonymic, see Lacan, "The Agency of the Letter in the Unconscious or Reason Since Freud," in *Ecrits*, pp. 146–78.

19. See, for instance, De Man, *Allegories of Reading*, and Krupnick, *Displacement*, an anthology of essays joined by this question.

20. See Jakobson and Halle, *Fundamentals of Language*, p. 80 ("A competition between both devices, metonymic and metaphoric, is manifest in any symbolic process, be it intrapersonal or social"); also see Jakobson, "Concluding Statement," p. 370 ("In poetry where similarity is superin-

duced upon contiguity, any metonymy is slightly metaphorical and any metaphor has a metonymical tint.").

21. Genette, "Métonymie chez Proust" in *Figures III*, pp. 41–63.

22. De Man, *Allegories of Reading*, pp. 3–19, 59–67.

23. Le Guern, *Sémantique*, pp. 19–20.

24. See Ricoeur, *La métaphore vive*, pp. 356–74, and De Man on the Romantic metaphor in "Structure intentionelle," pp. 68–84. Dante uses metaphor to suggest the divine not only throughout the *Commedia* but also in *La vita nuova* where, from the first sonnet, "Amor" signifies a divinely inspired presence as well as a human emotion.

25. Of this tendency to rely on previously set *topoi*, "Solo e pensoso" is an excellent example. Not only is a lone walk in nature a familiar classical and medieval theme, but many elements of the poem were most likely drawn from Propertius's "Haec certe deserte loci." As Wilkins has shown in *The Making of the Canzoniere*, pp. 295–98, it is Petrarch's subtle variations rather than the originality of theme that make his lyric unique.

26. Certain syntactic figures used by Petrarch, in particular the hyperbaton placing the verb at the end of the sentence, derive from classical patterns. See Rohlfs, *Historische Grammatik*, pp. 208–13.

27. Contini, *Varianti*, p. 173.

28. Augustine, *On Christian Doctrine*, pp. 34–35.

29. Bosco, *Francesco Petrarca*, pp. 24–53. This influential book first appeared in 1946.

30. See Laplanche and Pontalis, *The Language of Psychoanalysis*, p. 121. "The fact that an idea's emphasis, interest or intensity is liable to be detached from it and to pass on to other ideas, which were originally of little intensity but which are related to the first idea by a chain of associations . . ." opens their definition of displacement.

31. See Lacan, "The Agency," in *Ecrits*, esp. p. 156, for a discussion of desire and metonymy.

32. Benveniste, *Problèmes de linguistique générale*, pp. 228–36.

33. See Accademia della Crusca, *Concordanza*. By far the greatest number of substantives refer to either the world of nature or of myth.

34. The question was posed by Giacomo Colonna, one of Petrarch's closest friends. Petrarch responds:

> What in the world do you say? That I invented the splendid name of Laura so that it might be not only something for me to speak about but occasion to have others speak of me; that indeed there was no Laura on my mind except perhaps the poetic one for which I have aspired as is attested by my long and untiring studies. And finally you say that the truly live Laura by whose beauty I seem to be cap-

tured was completely invented, my poems fictitious and my sighs feigned. I wish indeed that you were joking about this particular subject, and that she indeed had been a fiction and not a madness!

Petrarca, *Rerum familiarum*, p. 102.

35. Petrarca, Introduction to *Petrarch's Lyric Poems*, translated and edited by Durling, p. 21.

36. Aristotle writes in the *Rhetoric*, ". . . we all take a natural pleasure in learning easily; so, since words stand for things, those words are most pleasing that give us fresh knowledge. Now strange words leave us in the dark; and current words [. . .] we know already. Accordingly, it is metaphor that is in the highest degree instructive and pleasing. When Homer calls old age 'stubble' [. . .], he makes us learn, gives us a new concept, by means of the common genus, since both things [old age and stubble] fall under the genus 'withered.'" Aristotle *Rhetoric* 3. 10. 1410b.

37. Particularly important are Petrarch's polemics against scholastic philosophy, whose emphases upon dialectic and natural philosophy most annoyed him. He attacks natural philosophy outright in two works: the *Invectiva contra medicum* and the *De sui ipsius et multorum ignorantia*. See Petrarca, *Opere latine*, 2:817–981, 1025–1151.

38. See "Posteritati," in Petrarca, *Prose*, p. 6. That Petrarch was not particularly proud of the limits of his understanding but fully resigned to them appears in the *Secretum*, *Prose*, pp. 22–215.

39. Trinkaus, *The Poet as Philosopher*, pp. 110–11. For a discussion of Petrarch's largely Ciceronian views on rhetoric and philosophy, see Seigel, *Rhetoric and Philosophy*, pp. 31–62.

40. Freccero, "The Fig Tree," pp. 37–40.

41. See De Man, *Allegories of Reading*, p. 18.

42. Greene, *The Light in Troy*, p. 124.

43. Petrarca, Introduction to *Petrarch's Lyric Poems*, translated and edited by Durling, pp. 18–33. See Greene, *The Light in Troy*, esp. pp. 104–46. Bosco, *Francesco Petrarca*, esp. pp. 54–67. Also Calcaterra, *Nella selva*, esp. pp. 10–24. Momigliano, *Storia*, esp. pp. 66–67.

44. Petrarca, *Rerum familiarum*, xxiv. l. 10, cited by Bosco, *Francesco Petrarca*, p. 57. (Translation mine.)

45. Petrarca, *Prose*, p. 611. The entire dialogue concerns the flight of time. (Translation mine.)

46. Petrarca, *Prose*, p. 94. (Translation mine.)

47. Calcaterra, *Nella selva*, p. 10; Bosco, *Francesco Petrarca*, p. 84.

48. Petrarca, *Prose*, pp. 146–48.

49. Ibid., pp. 1074–76.

50. See Mazzotta, "The 'Canzoniere,'" pp. 271–96, esp. p. 290.

51. Not only in Mazzotta, in "The 'Canzoniere,'" but also Waller, in

Petrarch's Poetics, see the Petrarchan "self" as problematic. See also Greene's discussion of search for self in *The Light in Troy*, pp. 104–26.

52. See Petrarca, Introduction to *Petrarch's Lyric Poems*, translated and edited by Durling, p. 11, for a comparison of the organization of the *Rime sparse* and the *Vita nuova*.

53. See Greene, *The Light in Troy*, pp. 112–13, for further comparisons with the epic.

54. Ibid., esp. pp. 81–103. For a more traditional discussion of Petrarch's knowledge of the classics, see Billanovitch, *Petrarca letterario*.

55. One of Petrarch's least personalized sonnets, it was one that was particularly appreciated by later sonnet writers. Cf. Edmund Spenser's "Like as a huntsman" and Thomas Wyatt's "Who so list to Hount" for different uses of the same "hunt of love" *topos*.

56. See Ducrot and Todorov, *Dictionnaire*, p. 378. [Translation mine.] Also Lévi-Strauss, *L'anthropologie structurale* I, pp. 227–55; esp. pp. 246, 248.

57. Nowhere is the semantic opening of "Una candida cerva" so evident as at the poem's closure: "quand'io caddi ne l'acqua et ella sparve." What is "l'acqua"? The Sorgue, the poet's tears, or a self-reflective surface? What sense ought to be attributed to "caddi"? The act of crying or a Narcissistic fall?

CHAPTER TWO

1. Shakespeare, *The Sonnets*, ed. Wilson, p. 46. I have quoted from this edition throughout.
2. Ibid., p. 191.
3. Leishman, *Themes and Variations*, p. 228.
4. Definitions are drawn from the *Oxford English Dictionary*.
5. See the discussion by Jakobson in Jakobson and Halle, *Fundamentals of Language*, p. 76; see also his "Concluding Statement," p. 358.
6. Day-Lewis, *The Poetic Image*, p. 72. Cf. Harries, "Metaphor and Transcendence," pp. 71–88.
7. Aristotle *Poetics* 21. 18. 1457b.
8. Nietzsche, "From 'On Truth and Lie in their Extramoral Sense,'" in *The Portable Nietzsche*, pp. 46–47:

> What, then, is truth? A mobile army of metaphors, metonyms and anthropomorphisms—in short, a sum of human relations, which have been enhanced, transposed and embellished poetically and rhetorically, and which after long use seem firm, canonical and obligatory to a people: truths are illusions about which one has forgotten that this is what they are; metaphors that are worn out and

without sensuous power; coins which have lost their pictures and now matter only as metal, not as coins.

9. Cf. Barthes, *S/Z*, pp. 16, 68–69.

10. See Elton, *The Tudor Constitution*, pp. 18–19.

11. Indeed, at times poets pursued Petrarchan rhetoric without the form. This is the case of early poets such as Antonio Tebaldeo (1463–1537), Serafino de' Cimminelli di Aquila (1466–1500) and Benedetto Gareth detto il Cariteo (died 1514), who often used the more epigrammatic form, the strambotto. For a full discussion of Petrarch's more important Italian imitators, see Baldacci, *Il Petrarchismo italiano*.

12. Pietro Bembo (1470–1547) revealed his mature Petrarchism in his *Rime*, his *Asolani* (in which several Petrarchan canzoni appear) and, above all, in the *Prose della volgare lingua*, where the literary language that Petrarch helped develop is analyzed and discussed. Giovanni Della Casa (1503–56) wrote sonnets with a *gravitas* that would later influence Milton. Michelangelo Buonarotti (1475–1564) authored a group of sonnets that, though less linguistically refined, tended to create effects more metaphysical in nature than those of any other Italian Renaissance poet.

13. Du Bellay, *Les regrets*, p. 239.

14. Puttenham, *The Arte of English Poesie*, p. 74.

15. The first edition of *Rime di diversi*, bk. 1, appeared in 1545; bk. 2 in 1547. See Scott, *Les sonnets elizabéthains*, p. 299.

16. See Castor, *Pléiade Poetics*, pp. 63–76.

17. The *Olive* appeared in 1549 and was greeted by accusations of plagiarism, so close did Du Bellay's translations stay to the Italian originals. In his second edition (1550), he responded to these charges. *Les antiquités de Rome* and *Les regrets* followed in 1558.

18. *Les amours* (de Cassandre) appeared in 1552; in 1555, *Continuation des amours* (Marie), and in 1556, *Nouvelle continuation des amours* (Hélène).

19. Javitch, *Poetry and Courtliness*. Javitch sees this emulation as proceeding in two directions:

> Puttenham considered the courtier as society's arbiter of style and proposed that the poet could perfect his verbal conduct by imitating proper court manners. But when the faith in exemplary courtliness waned a decade after Puttenham's *Arte* was written, this assumption was reversed. In the absence of any courtly models of comportment, the poet's special attributes (so similar to those of the courtier as he had been idealized) qualify *him* as society's maker of manners, and he emerges as the one who can impart lessons of conduct to the courtier. (p. 16)

20. Danby, *Poets on Fortune's Hill*, esp. pp. 21–45, and Melchiori, *Shakespeare's Dramatic Meditations*, pp. 12–13.

21. An excellent example is Wyatt's rendition of Petrarch's "Una Candida Cerva": "Who so list to Hount."

22. The dates and titles of the major sequences before Shakespeare's are these: Sir Philip Sidney, *Astrophil and Stella* (1591); Samuel Daniel, *Delia* (1592); Michael Drayton, *Ideas Mirror* (1594); Edmund Spenser, *Amoretti* (1595).

23. On the continuing enigma of the dating of Shakespeare's sonnets, see, for example, Schaar, *Elizabethan Sonnet Themes*.

24. Coleridge, *Table Talk*, pp. 275–76, quoted by S. Booth, *An Essay*, p. 158.

25. S. Booth, *An Essay*, p. 167.

26. Nowottney, "Formal Elements," p. 153.

27. Both Sir Thomas Wyatt and Henry, Earl of Surrey, wrote their poems between 1530 and 1540; the poems, however, were first published in 1557, in *Tottel's Miscellany*.

28. See esp. sonnets 67 and 68, but also 29, 33, 34, 37, 53, 62, and 63.

29. See, for example, sonnets 129, 133–34, 137–38, 141–42, 150, 152.

30. Krieger, in *A Window to Criticism*, develops this notion from a different critical perspective, with particular attention to the imagery of mirror and window.

31. See Donow, *Concordance*. See also Melchiori, *Shakespeare's Dramatic Meditations*, pp. 6–16, 197–200, who has made a statistical study of the sonnets.

32. Danby, *Poets on Fortune's Hill*, pp. 35–36.

33. There have been many readings and emendations of this sonnet's last lines. See S. Booth, for example, who examines a number of them in *Shakespeare's Sonnets*, pp. 368–69 ("No emendation or reading of line 14 recommends itself to the exclusion of the others.").

34. See esp. Lever, *The Elizabethan Sonnet Sequence*, pp. 172–73. On Shakespeare's dramatic lyricism in general, see also Lanham, *Motives of Eloquence*, pp. 111–28. In a somewhat different but related vein, Kennedy, in his *Rhetorical Norms*, pp. 57–78, offers some important insights into the dramatic qualities of Sidney's lyrics.

35. S. Booth, *Shakespeare's Sonnets*, p. 354.

36. S. Johnson, "Preface to Shakespeare," in *Johnson on Shakespeare*, p. 24.

37. Quoted in Mizener, "The Structure of Figurative Language," p. 137.

38. Muir, *Shakespeare's Sonnets*, contrasts the power of the sonnet with the feebleness of a scene from *Two Gentlemen of Verona*, pp. 128–29. S. Booth, in *Shakespeare's Sonnets*, pp. 199–200, and in *An Essay*, p. 66, merely refers to the poem's polyvalence.

39. Lanham, *A Handlist*, p. 71.

40. This is basically Adams's reading of the line as given in Shakespeare, *The Sonnets*, ed. Rollins, p. 114.

41. Pound, "How to Read," in *Literary Essays*, p. 25.
42. See, for instance, Herrnstein Smith, *Poetic Closure*, and S. Booth, *An Essay*, esp. p. 131.
43. Sonnets 5, 9, 24, 56, 63–64, 67–68, 94, 97, 105, 108, 121, 127, and 129 fit this nondramatic category. Technically, sonnet 44 belongs in this group, but it depends so heavily upon a preceding first person reference that it remains strangely personalized in spite of its third person form.
44. Though sonnet 20 has been cited as proof of Shakespeare's homosexuality, I would agree with S. Booth that this is indeed a careless reading of the poem. See S. Booth, *Shakespeare's Sonnets*, p. 163.
45. See, for instance, sonnets 21, 38, 78, 80, 82–85.
46. Constable, *The Poems*, p. 203.
47. Griffin, sonnet 39 of *Fidessa*, quoted by Hubler, "Shakespeare and the Unromantic Lady," p. 31.
48. Kristeva, *Séméiotiké*, p. 118; translation from Kristeva, p. 40.
49. Kristeva, *Séméiotiké*, pp. 119, 128.

CHAPTER THREE

1. Baudelaire, *Les fleurs du mal*, ed. Crépet and Blin, p. 17. I have quoted from this edition throughout.
2. Baudelaire, "Journaux intimes," in *Oeuvres complètes*, p. 1256. See also his essay on Victor Hugo, *Oeuvres complètes*, pp. 704–5.
3. Jakobson, "Concluding Statement," p. 358.
4. William Wordsworth, undated letter of 1833 to Dyce, quoted by Zillman, *John Keats and the Sonnet Tradition*, pp. 46–47.
5. Though the French sonnet had been renewed in the Baroque period, particularly in the work of Antoine-Gérard de Saint-Amant, it was also associated—much to its detriment—with the "précieux" poets of the seventeenth century, such as Vincent Voiture.
6. As Cassagne notes, the sonnet was beginning to become a more popular form among authors such as Théodore de Banville, Leconte de Lisle, and Joséphin Soulary. See *Versification et métrique*, pp. 89–90.
7. Baudelaire, "Salon de 1859," in *Oeuvres complètes*, p. 1043. (Translation mine.)
8. Morier, *Dictionnaire de poétique*, pp. 390–93.
9. See Baudelaire's essay on Victor Hugo, *Oeuvres complètes*, pp. 701–11.
10. See Fletcher, *Allegory*, esp. p. 16, and De Man, "The Rhetoric of Temporality," pp. 173–91. Both quote Coleridge extensively.
11. Lanham, *A Handlist*, pp. 61–62.
12. De Man, "The Rhetoric of Temporality," pp. 191–209.
13. Baudelaire, "De l'essence du rire et généralement du comique dans les arts plastiques," in *Oeuvres complètes*, p. 982.

14. De Man, "The Rhetoric of Temporality," pp. 206–7.
15. Ibid., p. 206.
16. Ibid., pp. 203–4.
17. Baudelaire, "De l'essence," in *Oeuvres complètes*, p. 985.
18. Ibid., pp. 982–83.
19. Ibid., p. 993.
20. Baudelaire, "Le poème du haschisch," in *Oeuvres complètes*, p. 376. Later, Baudelaire suggests the similarity between the culpable paradise of the smoker of hashish and the legitimate one of the poet, p. 387.
21. For the complex sources of this poem, see Baudelaire, *Les fleurs du mal*, ed. Crépet and Blin, pp. 316–17, and Baudelaire, *Les fleurs du mal*, ed. Adam, pp. 288–89.
22. Baudelaire, "Le peintre de la vie moderne," in *Oeuvres Complètes*, pp. 1152–92.
23. Benjamin, "The Work of Art in the Age of Mechanical Reproduction," in *Illuminations*, p. 221. Compare Ward-Jouve, *Baudelaire*, pp. 105–14.
24. Baudelaire, "Richard Wagner et *Tannhäuser* à Paris," in *Oeuvres Complètes*, pp. 1213–14.
25. Pound, "How to Read," in *Literary Essays*, p. 25.
26. See Bouverot, "Comparaison et métaphore," pp. 224–38.
27. Ducrot and Todorov, *Dictionnaire encyclopédique*, p. 358. See also Tesnière, *Syntaxe structurale*, p. 85.
28. That this sonnet might well be a sort of literary prank has been suggested by several scholars, including Adam, in Baudelaire, *Les fleurs du mal*, ed. Adam, pp. 360–61. If this is so, the effect of irony is only increased.
29. On the relationship of Baudelaire to Ronsard, see Cassou-Yager, *La polyvalence*, pp. 47–73. For a discussion of Baudelaire's tactics of sublimation, see B. Johnson, *Défigurations*, esp. pp. 31–55.
30. Cf. Jauss, "Il ricorso di Baudelaire," pp. 501–16.
31. See Benjamin, "On Some Motifs in Baudelaire," in *Illuminations*, pp. 168–70.
32. Baudelaire, "Le guignon," in *Les fleurs du mal*, ed. Crépet and Blin, p. 6.
33. Baudelaire, "Le peintre de la vie moderne," in *Oeuvres complètes*, p. 1163.
34. Baudelaire, "Salon de 1859," in *Oeuvres complètes*, pp. 1037–38.
35. Baudelaire, "L'art philosophique," in *Oeuvres complètes*, p. 1099.
36. Baudelaire, "Théophile Gautier," in *Oeuvres complètes*, p. 690.
37. Letter of Baudelaire (no date given), quoted by Cassagne, *Versification*, p. 90.
38. Baudelaire, "Salon de 1859," in *Oeuvres complètes*, p. 1037.
39. Mazzeo, *Renaissance and Seventeenth Century Studies*, p. 58.

40. See Merleau-Ponty, *Phénoménologie*, esp. pp. 240–80.
41. Baudelaire, "Salon de 1859," in *Oeuvres complètes*, p. 1038. See also Galand, "Baudelaire's Formulary," pp. 41–64 and Ward-Jouve, *Baudelaire*, esp. pp. 115–36 and 147–56.
42. Baudelaire, "Quelques caricaturistes étrangers," in *Oeuvres complètes*, p. 1018.
43. Freud, *The Interpretation of Dreams*, p. 319.
44. Ibid., pp. 277–79.
45. See Cargo, *A Concordance*, pp. 389–90.
46. Ibid.
47. Freud, *The Interpretation of Dreams*, p. 322. For a Freudian reading of the Baudelairean text and Baudelaire as a poet, see Bersani, *Baudelaire and Freud*.
48. Guiraud, *Essais de stylistique*, p. 96.
49. See especially "Obsession" and "Brumes et Pluies," in Baudelaire, *Les fleurs du mal*.
50. Freud, *The Interpretation of Dreams*, pp. 322–26.
51. Baudelaire, "Le poème du haschisch," in *Oeuvres complètes*, p. 354. Here, Baudelaire compares the effect of hashish to the "rêve naturel":

> L'ivresse, dans toute sa durée, ne sera, il est vrai, qu'un immense rêve, grâce à l'intensité des couleurs et à la rapidité des conceptions; mais elle gardera toujours la tonalité particulière de l'individu.

Somewhat later he writes:

> Par une équivoque singulière, par une espèce de transposition ou de quiproquo intellectuel, vous vous sentirez vous évaporant, et vous attribuerez à votre pipe (dans laquelle vous vous sentez accroupi et ramassé comme le tabac) l'étrange faculté de *vous fumer*. (p. 365)

52. Poulet, *Métamorphoses du cercle*, pp. 406–7.
53. Baudelaire, "Journaux intimes," in *Oeuvres complètes*, p. 1247.
54. Ibid., p. 1248.

CONCLUSION

1. See Ruthven, *Ezra Pound's Personae*, pp. 20–21.
2. W. R. Johnson, *The Idea of Lyric*, esp. p. 3.
3. Rogers, *The Three Genres*, pp. 9–76. See also the short article on "Lyric" in Preminger, *Princeton Encyclopedia*, pp. 460–70.
4. Plato *Republic* 3. 392–94; Coleridge, *Biographia literaria*, vol. 7 of *The Collected Works*; Jakobson, "Concluding Statement," p. 357.
5. Fussell, *Poetic Meter*, p. 126.
6. Berryman, *Berryman's Sonnets*, p. 75.
7. Rossetti, *The House of Life* in *The Collected Works*, p. 176.

Bibliography

Accademia della Crusca, ed. *Concordanza del 'Canzoniere' di Francesco Petrarca*. Florence: Accademia della Crusca, 1971.
Alighieri, Dante. *De vulgari eloquentia*. Translated by Aristide Marigo. Florence: Le Monnier, 1948.
_____. *La vita nuova*. Edited by Giovanni Melodia. Milano: Vallardi, 1905.
Aristotle. *The Rhetoric of Aristotle*. Translated by Lane Cooper. New York: D. Appleton and Co., 1932.
_____. *Aristotle's Poetics: A Translation and Commentary for Students of Literature*. Translated by Leon Golden. Englewood Cliffs, N.J.: Prentice-Hall, 1968.
Augustine, Saint. *On Christian Doctrine*. New York: The Liberal Arts Press, 1958.
Baldacci, Luigi. *Il Petrarchismo italiano nel cinquecento*. Milano: R. Ricciardi, 1957.
Barthes, Roland. *S/Z*. Paris: Editions du Seuil, 1970.
Baudelaire, Charles. *Les fleurs du mal*. Edited by Antoine Adam. Paris: Garnier, 1961.
_____. *Les fleurs du mal*. Edited by Jacques Crépet and Georges Blin. Paris: Corti, 1942.
_____. *Oeuvres complètes*. Edited by Y- G. Le Dantec and Claude Pichois. Paris: Gallimard, 1961.
Benjamin, Walter. *Illuminations*. Edited by Hannah Arendt. Translated by Harry Zohn. New York: Schocken Books, 1969.
Benveniste, Emile. *Problèmes de linguistique générale*. Paris: Gallimard, 1966.
Berni, Francesco. *Opere burlesche*. Roma: Jacomo Broedelat, 1771.
Berryman, John. *Berryman's Sonnets*. New York: Farrar, Straus and Giroux, 1967.

Bersani, Leo. *Baudelaire and Freud*. Berkeley: University of California Press, 1977.

Billanovitch, Giuseppe. *Petrarca letterario: Lo scrittoio del Petrarca*. Roma: Edizioni de "Storia e letteratura," 1947.

Booth, Stephen. *An Essay on Shakespeare's Sonnets*. New Haven: Yale University Press, 1969.

———. *Shakespeare's Sonnets*. New Haven: Yale University Press, 1977.

Booth, Wayne. "Metaphor as Rhetoric: The Problem of Evaluation." In *On Metaphor*, edited by Sheldon Sacks, pp. 47–70. Chicago: University of Chicago Press, 1978.

Bosco, Umberto. *Francesco Petrarca*. Bari: Laterza, 1961.

Bouverot, Danielle. "Comparaison et métaphore." *Le Français moderne* 37 (1969): 132–47, 224–38, 301–16.

Calcaterra, Carlo. *Nella selva del Petrarca*. Bologna: Cappelli, 1942.

Cargo, Robert T. *A Concordance to Baudelaire's "Les Fleurs du Mal."* Chapel Hill: University of North Carolina Press, 1965.

Cassagne, Albert. *Versification et métrique de Charles Baudelaire*. Paris: Librairie Hachette, 1906.

Cassou-Yager, Hélène. *La polyvalence du thème de la mort dans "Les Fleurs du Mal" de Baudelaire*. Paris: A. G. Nizet, 1979.

Castor, Grahame. *Pléiade Poetics: A Study in Sixteenth Century Thought and Terminology*. Cambridge: Cambridge University Press, 1964.

Coleridge, Samuel Taylor. *The Collected Works of Samuel Taylor Coleridge*. Edited by Kathleen Coburn. 13 vols. London: Routledge and Kegan Paul, 1969.

———. *The Table Talk and Omniana*. Edited by T. Ashe. London: G. Bell and Sons, 1923.

Constable, Henry. *The Poems of Henry Constable*. Edited by Joan Grundy. Liverpool: Liverpool University Press, 1960.

Contini, Gianfranco. *Varianti e altra linguistica*. Torino: Einaudi, 1970.

Danby, John. *Poets on Fortune's Hill*. London: Faber and Faber, 1952.

Day-Lewis, C. *The Poetic Image*. London: Cape, 1947.

De Man, Paul. *Allegories of Reading*. New Haven: Yale University Press, 1979.

———. "The Rhetoric of Temporality." In *Interpretation, Theory and Practice*, edited by Charles S. Singleton, pp. 173–209. Baltimore: Johns Hopkins University Press, 1961.

———. "Structure intentionelle de l'image romantique." *Revue Internationale de Philosophie* 51 (1960): 68–84.

Derrida, Jacques. *De la grammatologie*. Paris: Editions de Minuit, 1967.

Donow, Herbert S. *A Concordance to the Sonnet Sequences of Daniel, Drayton, Shakespeare, Sidney and Spenser*. Carbondale: Southern Illinois University Press, 1969.

Du Bellay, Joachim. *Les regrets, Les antiquités de Rome et La défense et illustration de la langue Française*. Paris: Gallimard, 1967.
Ducrot, Oswald, and Todorov, Tzvetan. *Dictionnaire encyclopédique des sciences du langage*. Paris: Seuil, 1972.
Elton, G. R. *The Tudor Constitution*. Cambridge: Cambridge University Press, 1960.
Ferrante, Joan, and Economou, George, eds. *In Pursuit of Perfection: Courtly Love in Medieval Literature*. New York: Kennikat Press, 1975.
Fletcher, Angus. *Allegory: The Theory of a Symbolic Mode*. Ithaca, N.Y.: Cornell University Press, 1964.
Freccero, John. "The Fig Tree and the Laurel: Petrarch's Poetics." *Diacritics* 5 (1975): 34–40.
Freud, Sigmund. *The Interpretation of Dreams*. Translated and edited by James Strachey. New York: Basic Books, 1955.
Fussell, Paul. *Poetic Meter and Poetic Form*. Rev. ed. New York: Random House, 1979.
Galand, René. "Baudelaire's Formulary of the True Esthetics." In *Baudelaire as a Love Poet*, edited by Lois Boe Hyslop, pp. 41–64. University Park: Pennsylvania State University Press, 1969.
Genette, Gerard. *Figures III*. Paris: Seuil, 1972.
Greene, Thomas M. *The Light in Troy: Imitation and Discovery in Renaissance Poetry*. New Haven: Yale University Press, 1982.
Guiraud, Pierre. *Essais de stylistique*. Paris: Klincksieck, 1969.
Harries, Karston. "Metaphor and Transcendence." In *On Metaphor*, edited by Sheldon Sacks, pp. 71–88. Chicago: University of Chicago Press, 1979.
Herrnstein Smith, Barbara. *Poetic Closure: A Study of How Poems End*. Chicago: University of Chicago Press, 1968.
Hubler, Edward. "Shakespeare and the Unromantic Lady." In *Discussions of Shakespeare's Sonnets*, edited by Barbara Herrnstein Smith, pp. 28–45. Boston: Heath and Co., 1964.
Jakobson, Roman. "Concluding Statement: Linguistics and Poetics." In *Style in Language*, edited by Thomas Sebeok, pp. 350–77. Cambridge: Massachusetts Institute of Technology Press, 1960.
Jakobson, Roman, and Halle, Morris. *Fundamentals of Language*. The Hague: Mouton, 1956.
Jauss, Hans Robert. "Il ricorso di Baudelaire all' allegoria." *Belfagor* 5 (1980): 501–16.
Javitch, Daniel. *Poetry and Courtliness in Renaissance England*. Princeton: Princeton University Press, 1978.
Johnson, Barbara. *Défigurations du langage poétique*. Paris: Flammarion, 1979.
Johnson, Samuel. *Johnson on Shakespeare*. Edited by Walter Raleigh. Lon-

don: Oxford University Press, 1925.
Johnson, W. R. *The Idea of Lyric: Lyric Modes in Ancient and Modern Poetry.* Berkeley: University of California Press, 1982.
Kennedy, William J. *Rhetorical Norms in Renaissance Literature.* New Haven: Yale University Press, 1978.
Krieger, Murray. *A Window to Criticism: Shakespeare's Sonnets and Modern Poetics.* Princeton: Princeton University Press, 1964.
Kristeva, Julia. *Desire in Language: A Semiotic Approach to Literature and Art.* Edited by Leon Roudiez. New York: Columbia University Press, 1980.
———. *Séméiotiké: Recherches pour une sémanalyse.* Paris: Seuil, 1969.
Krupnick, Mark, ed. *Displacement: Derrida and After.* Bloomington: Indiana University Press, 1983.
Lacan, Jacques. *Ecrits: A Selection.* Translated by Alan Sheridan. New York: Norton, 1977.
Lanham, Richard A. *A Handlist of Rhetorical Terms.* Berkeley: University of California Press, 1969.
———. *Motives of Eloquence. Literary Rhetoric in the Renaissance.* New Haven: Yale University Press, 1976.
Laplanche, Jean, and Pontalis, J. B. *The Language of Psychoanalysis.* Translated by Donald Nicholson-Smith. London: Hogarth Press, 1973.
Le Guern, Michel. *Sémantique de la métaphore et de la métonymie.* Paris: Larousse, 1973.
Leishman, J. B. *Themes and Variations in Shakespeare's Sonnets.* London: Hutchinson and Co., 1961.
Leopardi, Giacomo, ed. *Rime di Francesco Petrarca.* Milano: Sonzogno, 1893.
Lever, J. W. *The Elizabethan Sonnet Sequence.* London: Methuen and Co., 1956.
Lévi-Strauss, Claude. *L'anthropologie structurale.* 2 vols. Paris: Plon, 1958.
Mazzeo, Joseph. *Renaissance and Seventeenth Century Studies.* New York: Columbia University Press, 1964.
Mazzotta, Guiseppe. "The 'Canzoniere' and the Language of the Self." *Studies in Philology* 75 (1978): 271–96.
Melchiori, Giorgio. *Shakespeare's Dramatic Meditations: An Experiment in Criticism.* Oxford: Clarendon Press, 1976.
Merleau-Ponty, Maurice. *Phénoménologie de la perception.* Paris: Gallimard, 1945.
Mizener, Arthur. "The Structure of Figurative Language in Shakespeare's Sonnets." In *Discussions of Shakespeare's Sonnets,* edited by Barbara Herrnstein Smith, pp. 137–51. Boston: Heath and Co., 1964.
Momigliano, Attilio. *Storia della letteratura italiana.* Messina: Principato, 1938.

Mönch, Walter. *Das Sonett: Gestalt und Geschichte*. Heidelberg: F. H. Kerle, 1955.
Morier, Henri. *Dictionnaire de poétique et de rhétorique*. Paris: Presses Universitaires de France, 1961.
Muir, Kenneth. *Shakespeare's Sonnets*. London: George Allen and Unwin, 1979.
Nietzsche, Friedrich. *The Portable Nietzsche*. Translated by Walter Kaufman. New York: Penguin, 1976.
Nowottney, Winifred. "Formal Elements in Shakespeare's Sonnets I–VI." In *Discussions of Shakespeare's Sonnets*, edited by Barbara Herrnstein Smith, pp. 152–58. Boston: Heath and Co., 1964.
Oppenheimer, Paul. "The Origin of the Sonnet." *Comparative Literature* 34 (1982): 289–304.
Oxford English Dictionary. Oxford: Oxford University Press, 1971.
Petrarca, Francesco. *Canzoniere*. Edited by Gianfranco Contini. Torino: Einaudi, 1966.
———. *Opere latine*. Edited by Antonietta Bufano. 2 vols. Torino: Unione tipografico-editrice torinese, 1975.
———. *Petrarch's Lyric Poems*. Translated and edited by Robert M. Durling. Cambridge: Harvard University Press, 1976.
———. *Prose*. Edited by G. Martelloti, P. G. Ricci, E. Carrara, and E. Bianchi. Milano: Ricciardi, 1955.
———. *Rerum familiarum libri I–VIII*. Translated by Aldo S. Bernardo. Albany: State University of New York Press, 1975.
Plato. *The Republic of Plato*. Translated by Francis MacDonald Cornford. New York: Oxford University Press, 1945.
Poulet, Georges. *Métamorphoses du cercle*. Paris: Plon, 1961.
Pound, Ezra. *Literary Essays*. Edited by T. S. Eliot. Norfolk, Conn.: New Directions, 1954.
Preminger, Alex, ed. *Princeton Encyclopedia of Poetry and Poetics*. Princeton: Princeton University Press, 1965.
Puttenham, Richard. *The Arte of English Poesie*. Facsimile reproduction. Kent, Ohio: Kent State University Press, 1970.
Ricoeur, Paul. *La métaphore vive*. Paris: Seuil, 1975.
Riffaterre, Michael. *Semiotics of Poetry*. Bloomington: Indiana University Press, 1978.
Rogers, William Elford. *The Three Genres and the Interpretation of Lyric*. Princeton: Princeton University Press, 1983.
Rohlfs, Gerhardt. *Historische Grammatik der Italienischen Sprache und ihrer Mundarten*. Bern: A. Franck, 1954.
Rossetti, Dante Gabriel. *The Collected Works of Dante Gabriel Rossetti*. Edited by William Rossetti. London: Ellis and Elvey, 1887.
Ruthven, R. K. *A Guide to Ezra Pound's Personae, 1926*. Berkeley: Univer-

sity of California Press, 1969.
Sapegno, Natalino. *Disegno storico della letteratura Italiana*. Florence: La Nuova Italia, 1966.
Schaar, Claes. *Elizabethan Sonnet Themes and the Dating of Shakespeare's Sonnets*. New York: AMS Press, 1973.
Scott, Janet C. *Les sonnets Elizabéthains*. Paris: Librairie Ancienne Honoré Champion, 1929.
Seigel, Jerrold. *Rhetoric and Philosophy in Renaissance Humanism: The Union of Eloquence and Wisdom, Petrarch to Valla*. Princeton: Princeton University Press, 1968.
Shakespeare, William. *The Sonnets*. Edited by Hyder E. Rollins. Philadelphia and London: J. P. Lippincott Co., 1944.
―――. *The Sonnets*. Edited by John Dover Wilson. London: Cambridge University Press, 1966.
Sonnino, Lee A. *A Handbook to Sixteenth Century Rhetoric*. London: Routledge and Kegan Paul, 1968.
Tesnière, Lucien. *Eléments de syntaxe structurale*. Paris: Klincksieck, 1959.
Trinkaus, Charles. *The Poet as Philosopher: Petrarch and the Formation of Renaissance Consciousness*. New Haven: Yale University Press, 1979.
Vellutello, Alessandro. *Il Petrarca*. Venice: Gabriele Giolito de Ferrari, 1558.
Waller, Marguerite. *Petrarch's Poetics and Literary History*. Amherst: University of Massachusetts Press, 1980.
Ward-Jouve, Nicole. *Baudelaire: A Fire to Conquer Darkness*. London: Macmillan Press, 1980.
Wilkins, Ernst Hatch. *The Invention of the Sonnet and Other Studies in Italian Literature*. Roma: Edizioni di Storia e Letteratura, 1959.
―――. *The Making of the Canzoniere and Other Petrarchan Studies*. Roma: Edizioni di Storia e Letteratura, 1951.
Zillman, Lawrence. *John Keats and the Sonnet Tradition: A Critical and Comparative Study*. Los Angeles: Lymanhouse, 1939.

Index

Alfieri, Vittorio, 91
Alighieri, Dante, 143; *Divina Commedia*, 15, 23; metaphor and allegory in, 21, 37; *Rime petrose*, 14; sonnet and canzone compared in *De vulgari eloquentia*, 14; *Vita nuova*, 14–15
Allegory and irony: in Baudelairean sonnet, 6, 100–109, 113, 120–21, 144; in Dante, 37; use by Baudelaire compared to Dante, 104
Alliteration and assonance, 32–33, 43
Analogy: in Baudelairean sonnet, 94–96, 128, 132–33; related to metaphor, 94, 128; in traditional verse form, 94
Anaphora, 112–13
Antithesis, 34
Aristotle, 35, 54, 156 (n. 36)
Auden, W. H., 149
Augustine, Saint, 12, 24, 40
"Aura," 107

Baif, Jean Antoine de, 59
Baudelaire, Charles, 91, 97–100, 131–32; "De l'essence du rire," 101; *Les fleurs du mal*, 4, 94, 100, 103, 107, 120–23, 127, 131, 134, 136, 138, 144; "Le peintre de la vie moderne," 106, 123; "Le poème du haschisch," 104, 161 (n. 20), 162 (n. 51); "Richard Wagner et *Tannhäuser* à Paris," 107–8; "Salon de 1859," 128
—Individual poems from *Les fleurs du mal*: "A une passante" (93), 122; "Avec ses vêtements ondoyants et nacrés" (27), 111; "Les aveugles" (92), 122, 125, 127; "La beauté" (17), 111; "Les bijoux" (127), 116–19, 125; "Brumes et pluies" (101), 122; "Le cadre" (38:III), 118–19; "La chevelure" (23), 94; "Correspondances" (4), 94, 111, 120, 128–31, 133, 137, 140; "La destruction" (109), 122; "Les deux bonnes soeurs" (112), 122; "Un fantôme" (38), 118; "Le flambeau vivant" (43), 111–13, 115, 133, 140; "La fontaine de sang" (113), 122; "L'invitation au voyage" (53), 94; "Je t'adore à l'égal de la voûte nocturne" (24), 115; "La mort des amants" (121), 126–28, 133; "La mort des pauvres"

(122), 122; "Le mort joyeux" (72), 114–15, 125, 161 (n. 28); "La musique" (69), 109–11, 113, 120, 133, 140; "Parfum exotique" (22), 94, 118; "La pipe" (68), 121, 135–38; "Le rêve d'un curieux" (125), 123; "Le revenant" (63), 125, 127; "Sonnet d'automne" (64), 104; "Spleen" (75), 104, 121–22, 133, 140; "La vie antérieure" (12), 93–96, 104–6, 120, 133, 140; "Le voyage" (126), 123, 125

Baudelairean sonnet: allegory and irony in, 6, 100–109, 113, 120–21, 144; analogy in, 94–96, 128, 132–33; anaphora in, 112–13; and "aura," 107; compared to predecessors, 8, 91, 95–100, 105, 107, 113–21, 127, 132, 134, 140–41, 144–49; and death, 114–15, 122–23, 126–27; and earthly paradise, 105; erotic in, 115–20; form of, 4, 97–99, 107, 113–14, 124–25, 133, 140, 142, 148–49; and imagination, 123–24, 128, 131; lexicon of, 134–35; and linguistic transcendence, 123–27; metaphor and simile in, 94–96, 100, 109–10, 128–29; parody in, 115; as "phanopoetic," 108; and "poésie pure," 96, 106; and rhetorical tradition, 99; and "sorcellerie évocatoire," 124–25; spatial quality of, 97, 107–11, 119, 132, 139, 144; split, ironic self in, 96, 100, 103–6, 120–22, 127–28, 132, 136–41, 145–46; and structure of dream, 132–38; and "surnaturel," 96, 113, 133; and synesthesia, 129–30

Belleau, Rémy, 59
Bembo, Pietro, 57, 158 (n. 12)
Benjamin, Walter, 107
Benveniste, Emile, 26

Berni, Francesco, 17, 86
Berryman, John, 150–51; *Berryman's Sonnets*, 150
Booth, Stephen, 64, 78–79
Bosco, Umberto, 25, 39
Browning, Elizabeth Barrett, 91
Buonarotti, Michelangelo, 57, 158 (n. 12)

Calcaterra, Carlo, 39
Cavalcanti, Guido, 14
Coleridge, Samuel Taylor, 64, 98, 145, 147; *Biographia Literaria*, 147
Constable, Henry, 87
Contini, Gianfranco, 12
Correspondences, theory of, 128–29
Courtly love, 13–14, 22, 85, 153–54 (n. 8)

Daniel, Samuel, 61, 73
Daubran, Marie, 115, 120
Davies, Sir John, 86
Day Lewis, C., 54
Delacroix, Eugène, 131
Della Casa, Giovanni, 57, 91, 158 (n. 12)
De Man, Paul, 20, 101–2, 105; *Allegories of Reading*, 20
De Sanctis, Francesco, 17
Descartes, René, 90
Displacement, 26, 155 (n. 30)
"Dolce stil novo," 14
Donne, John, 86, 91; *Holy Sonnets*, 91
Drayton, Michael, 73–74
Du Bellay, Joachim, 58–60, 86; *Antiquités de Rome*, 60; *Défense et illustration de la langue Française*, 58; *Olive*, 60, 158 (n. 17); *Regrets*, 60
Durling, Robert, 15, 31
Duval, Jeanne, 120

170 / Index

Eliot, T. S., 141, 146

Foscolo, Ugo, 91
Fourier, Charles, 128
Freccero, John, 38
Frederick II: court of, 13
Frénaud, André, 151
Freud, Sigmund, 19, 132, 134, 136; *Interpretation of Dreams*, 19
Fussell, Paul, 147

Gautier, Théophile, 91, 99
Genette, Gérard, 20
Gianni, Lappo, 14
Ginsberg, Allen, 151
Greene, Thomas, 38, 44
Griffin, Bartholomew, 88
Guinizelli, Guido, 14
Guiraud, Pierre, 136–37

Heaney, Seamus, 151
Hopkins, Gerard Manley, 149
Hugo, Victor, 98, 105; *Les rayons et les ombres*, 105

Identification (rhetorical), 109
Imagination, 123–24, 128, 131
Irony. *See* Allegory and irony

Jaccottet, Philippe, 151
Jakobson, Roman, 18–20, 54–55, 154–55 (n. 20)
Javitch, Daniel, 158 (n. 19)
Jodelle, Estienne, 59
Johnson, Samuel, 79

Keats, John, 91, 98
Kristeva, Julia, 89

Laura (in *Rime sparse*), 23–31, 39–40, 48, 155–56 (n. 34). *See also* Petrarchan sonnet
Leishman, J. B., 52
Lentino, Giacomo da, 13, 143

Logopoeia, 82, 145
Lyric, 98, 100, 146–47

Mallarmé, Stéphane, 141, 149
Marot, Clément, 59
Melopoeia, 145
Meredith, George, 149
Metaphor: associated with allegory and irony, 100; associated with lyric, 6, 17–19; associated with paradox and pun, 79–83, 144; and the "cognitive," 18; defined by Aristotle, 54, 156 (n. 36); defined by Day Lewis, 54; defined by Jakobson, 18–19; and metonymy, 18–20, 154–55 (n. 20). *See also* Baudelairean sonnet; Petrarchan sonnet; Shakespearean sonnet
Metonymy: defined by Jakobson, 18–20; and desire, 19; and metaphor, 18–20, 154–55 (n.20); and "performative," 19, 36. *See also* Petrarchan sonnet; Shakespearean sonnet
Morier, Henri, 99; *Dictionnaire de poétique et de rhétorique*, 99
Musset, Alfred de, 99
Myth, 28, 48–49. *See also* Petrarchan sonnet

Nerval, Gérard de, 91, 99
Nietzsche, Friedrich, 55, 157–58 (n. 8)
Nowottney, Winifred, 66

Oppenheimer, Paul, 5

Parody, 86–89, 115
Paronomasia, 25
Petrarch, Francesco, 12, 15, 37–40; *De remediis*, 39; *Rime sparse*, 4, 20, 26, 31, 35–42, 45, 58–59, 75, 117, 144, 146, 148; *Secretum*, 12,

39–40; *Seniles*, 40; "Trionfo dell'eternitá," 40
—Individual poems from the *Rime sparse*: "Anima bella da quel nodo sciolta" (305), 42; "Apollo, s'anchor vive il bel desio" (34), 28; "Benedetto sia 'l giorno e 'l mese et l'anno" (61), 42; "Chiare, fresche et dolci acque" (126), 27; "Di dí in dí vo cangiando il viso e 'l pelo" (195), 39; "Erano i capei d'oro a l'aura sparsi" (90), 42–46, 49; "Giovene donna sotto un verde lauro" (30), 29; "I begli occhi ond' i' fui percosso" (75), 27; "Il figliuol di Latona avea già nove" (43), 28; "I' vo pensando, et nel pensier m'assale" (264), 11–12; "Lasso, ben so che dolorose prede" (101), 39; "L'aura che 'l verde lauro et l'aureo crine" (246), 23, 25, 30, 45–47; "La vita fugge e non s'arresta una hora" (272), 39; "Lieti fiori et felici, et ben nate herbe" (162), 27; "Nel dolce tempo de la prima etade" (23), 41; "O bella man, che mi destringi 'l core" (199), 27; "Onde tolse Amor l'oro, et di qual vena" (220), 28; "Pace non trovo, et non ò da far guerra" (134), 33–35, 46, 87; "Padre del ciel, dopo i perduti giorni" (62), 42; "Quanti più m'avicino al giorno estremo" (32), 39; "Quel sol che mi mostrava il camin destro" (306), 42; "Sento l'aura mia anticha, e i dolci colli" (320), 28; "Solo e pensoso i più deserti campi" (35), 10–12, 20–23, 32, 35, 45; "Una candida cerva sopra l'erba" (190), 47–49, 157 (n. 57); "Voi ch'ascoltate in rime sparse il suono" (l), 31–33, 45–46; "Volo con l'ali de' pensieri al cielo" (362), 114

Petrarchan sonnet: and allegory, 37; alliteration and assonance in, 32–33, 43; and antithesis, 34; and classical inspiration, 15, 22–24, 37–39, 44, 143; compared to myth, 47–50; form of, 1–3, 13–15, 45–50, 142–43; grammar and syntax of, 17–23, 32–35, 38, 45, 142; "hunt of love" and desire in, 19, 30, 39–40, 47–49, 142; and Laura, 23–31, 39–40, 48, 155–56 (n. 34); and literary history, 8, 13–15, 44, 49–50, 57–62, 143, 155 (n. 25), 157 (n. 55); and metaphor, 17–21, 28, 35–36, 44–45; and metonymy, 6, 18–23, 25–28, 36–38, 43, 45, 142; and poetic voice, 5, 16, 22–23, 29–36, 38–50, 142–43, 146; and transience, 38–39

Phanopoeia, 108, 145
Plato, 147; *Republic*, 147
Pléiade, 58–60, 114
Poe, Edgar Allan, 131
Poulet, Georges, 139
Pound, Ezra, 82, 108, 145
Propertius, Sextus, 57, 155 (n. 25)
Proust, Marcel, 135
Pun and paradox, 79–83, 144
Puttenham, Richard, 58

Rich, Adrienne, 151
Rilke, Rainer Maria, 149
Rime di diversi, 59
Ronsard, Pierre de, 59–60, 114; *Amours*, 60
Rosetti, Dante Gabriel, 151
Rousseau, Jean Jacques, 105

Sabatier, Apollonie-Aglaé, 120
Saint-Amant, Antoine-Gérard de, 160 (n. 5)
Sainte-Beuve, Charles Augustin, 99
Saint-Gelais, Mellin de, 59
Saussure, Ferdinand de, 18
"Scuola siciliana," 13
Shakespeare, William, 74, 78; *Love's Labour's Lost*, 86; *Romeo and Juliet*, 85; *Sonnets*, 4, 58, 61–62, 69–74, 76, 84–85, 89, 91, 143–44, 146; *The Two Gentlemen of Verona*, 85–86

—Individual sonnets: "Alas 'tis true, I have gone here and there" (110), 78; "As fast as thou shalt wane so fast thou grow'st" (11), 69; "But wherefore do you not a mightier way" (16), 70; "Devouring Time blunt thou the lion's paws" (19), 114; "Farewell! thou art too dear for my possessing" (87), 51–54, 56–57, 62–65, 77, 85; "For shame deny that thou bear'st love to any" (10), 70; "From fairest creatures we desire increase" (1), 66–69, 72, 85; "Is it for fear to wet a widow's eye" (9), 70; "Like as the waves make towards the pebbled shore" (60), 71; "Look in thy glass and tell the face thou viewest" (3), 69; "My mistress' eyes are nothing like the sun" (130), 86–88; "O for my sake do you with Fortune chide" (111), 78; "O never say that I was false of heart" (109), 78; "Shall I compare thee to a summer's day?" (18), 71; "Since brass, nor stone, nor earth, nor boundless sea" (65), 71; "Take all my loves, my love, yea take them all" (40), 79–83, 85; "That thou hast her it is not all my grief" (42), 79; "That time of year thou mayst in me behold" (73), 72; "Unthrifty loveliness why dost thou spend" (4), 69; "Was it the proud full sail of his great verse" (86), 52; "Whoever hath her wish, thou hast thy will" (135), 79; "Your love and pity doth th'impression fill" (112), 75–78, 85

Shakespearean sonnet: ambiguity in, 53, 61, 79–83, 144; "cognitive" and "performative" in, 52, 66, 73, 84; compared to Petrarchan sonnet, 62, 65, 73, 75, 83–85, 89, 142–44; drama in, 52–53, 62, 73–78, 83–84, 90, 143–44, 146; form of, 2, 4, 61, 67–69, 72, 83–85, 142–44; grammar and syntax in, 52–54, 65, 67–68; irony in, 62–64; lexicon of, 75; and *logopoeia*, 82, 145; metaphor and mimesis in, 6, 54–56, 64–67, 72, 79–83, 143–44; metonymy subordinate in, 65–67; parody in, 86–89; puns and paradox in, 79–83, 144; and reincarnation of poetic self, 70–72, 76–77; and Renaissance conventions, 57–62, 85–89; and sexual love, 71, 85; and theme of narcissism, 69–70

Sidney, Sir Phillip, 61, 68, 73–74, 143; *Astrophil and Stella*, 61, 143

Simile, 109–10

Sonnet, history of, 6–9, 142–45; anti-Petrarchism in, 85–88; and earliest examples of form, 3, 13–15; in eighteenth and nineteenth centuries, 91–92, 96–100, 107, 113–14, 144–45, 148–49; in modern and contemporary poetry,

141, 149–51; and Renaissance poetry, 49–50, 57–62, 67–68, 73–74, 90–91, 143–44, 148, 158 (nn. 11, 12). *See also* Baudelairean sonnet; Petrarchan sonnet; Shakespearean sonnet

Sonnet form, 1–7, 58–62, 99–100, 113–14, 142, 146–50. *See also* Baudelairean sonnet; Petrarchan sonnet; Shakespearean sonnet

"Sorcellerie évocatoire," 94, 124–25

Spenser, Edmund, 61, 68, 73–74, 143, 157 (n. 55); *Amoretti*, 143

Sponde, Jean de, 60

Stevens (critic of Shakespeare), 79

Stevens, Wallace, 149

"Surnaturel," 96, 113

Surrealists, 141

Surrey, Henry Howard, Earl of, 58, 60–61, 67–68, 74

Swedenborg, Emanuel, 128

Symbolists, 141
Synesthesia, 129–30

Tyard, Pontus de, 59

Unilinguismo, 22

Valéry, Paul, 141
Vergil, 44; *Aeneid*, 44
Verlaine, Paul, 141
Versification. *See* Baudelairean sonnet; Petrarchan sonnet; Shakespearean sonnet; Sonnet form
Virgin Mary, 40
Voiture, Vincent, 160 (n. 5)

Wilson, John Dover, 52
Wordsworth, William, 91, 97–98
Wyatt, Sir Thomas, 58, 60–61, 74, 157 (n. 55)